Stephen Sharkey

The May Queen

Published by Methuen Drama 2007

1 3 5 7 9 10 8 6 4 2

Methuen Drama
A & C Black Publishers Limited
38 Soho Square
London W1D 3HB
www.acblack.com

ISBN: 978 0 713 68714 9

A CIP catalogue record for this book
is available from the British Library

Typeset by Country Setting, Kingsdown, Kent
Printed in the UK by CPI Bookmarque, Croydon, CR0 4TD

Caution

This book is produced using paper that is made from wood grown
in managed, sustainable forests. It is natural, renewable and recyclable.
The logging and manufacturing processes conform to the environmental
regulations of the country of origin.

Liverpool Everyman and Playhouse present the world première of

The May Queen

by Stephen Sharkey

First performed on 4 May 2007 at the Everyman Theatre, Liverpool

Liverpool Everyman and Playhouse
About the Theatres

As Liverpool prepares to take on the mantle of European Capital of Culture in 2008, the Everyman and Playhouse are experiencing a dramatic upsurge in creative activity. Since January 2004, we have been continually in production, creating shows which have ensured that 'Made In Liverpool' is widely recognised as a stamp of theatrical quality once again.

Around our in-house productions, we host some of the finest touring companies from around the country, to offer a rich and varied programme for the people of Liverpool and Merseyside, and for the increasing number of visitors to our city.

But there is more to these theatres than simply the work on our stages. We have a busy Literary Department, working to nurture the next generation of Liverpool Playwrights. A wide-ranging community department takes our work to all corners of the city and surrounding areas, and works in partnership with schools, colleges, youth and community groups to open up the theatre to all.

Our aim is for these theatres to be an engine for creative excellence, artistic adventure, and audience involvement; firmly rooted in our community, yet both national and international in scope and ambition.

"The two theatres have undergone a remarkable renaissance... Liverpool's theatreland has not looked so good in years" Daily Post

13 Hope Street, Liverpool, L1 9BH
www.everymanplayhouse.com
Company Registration No. 3802476 Registered Charity No. 1081229

Liverpool Everyman and Playhouse would like to thanks all our current funders:

Corporate Members A C Robinson and Associates, Barbara McVey, Beetham Organisation, Benson Signs, Brabners Chaffe Street, Chadwick Chartered Accountants, Concept Communications, Downtown Liverpool in Business, Duncan Sheard Glass, DWF Solicitors, EEF NorthWest, Grant Thornton, Hope Street Hotel, Lewis's, Mando Group, Morgenrot Chevaliers, Radio City 96.7, Synergy Colour Printing, The Mersey Partnership, Victor Huglin Carpets.

Trusts & Foundations The PH Holt Charitable Trust, The Eleanor Rathbone Charitable Trust, The Granada Foundation, The Lynn Foundation, The Peggy Ramsay Foundation, Liverpool Culture Company, The Rex Makin Charitable Trust, The Golsoncott Foundation, The Pilkington General Fund, The Harry Pilkington Trust, The Garrick Trust, The Julia Marmor Trust, The Ernest Cook Trust, The Penny Cress Charitable Trust, Malcolm and Roger Frood in memory of Graham and Joan Frood, The Helen Hamlyn Foundation, E Alec Coleman Charitable Trust, Duchy of Lancaster Benevolent Fund.

And our growing number of individual supporters.

New Writing at the Liverpool Everyman and Playhouse

"The Everyman is back producing the next generation of Liverpool playwrights."
(The Guardian)

At the beating heart of the theatre's renaissance is our work with writers; since it is our passionate belief that an investment in new writing is an investment in our theatrical future.

The May Queen is the latest in a rich and varied slate of world, european and regional premières which has been enthusiastically received by Merseyside audiences and helped to put Liverpool's theatre back on the national map.

"The Everyman in Liverpool is living up to its name. Thanks to a new play, it is doing what theatres all over the country dream of: pulling in scores of first time theatre goers alongside loyal subscribers... blazes with energetic intelligence... this will change people's minds and in unexpected ways." (The Observer on *Unprotected*)

In just over two years, the theatres will have produced ten world premières of plays developed and nurtured in Liverpool - most recently including *The Electric Hills* by Michael McLean, *The Flint Street Nativity* by Tim Firth, *The Way Home* by Chloë Moss, *Paradise Bound* by Jonathan Larkin and *Unprotected* by Esther Wilson, John Fay, Tony Green and Lizzie Nunnery, which transferred to the Edinburgh Festival where it won the Amnesty International Freedom of Expression Award.

"A remarkable renaissance." (Liverpool Daily Post)

Other highly acclaimed productions have included the European première of *Yellowman* by Dael Orlandersmith, which transferred to Hampstead Theatre and successfully toured nationally, and regional premières of Conor McPherson's *Port Authority*, Simon Block's *Chimps* and Gregory Burke's *On Tour* - a co-production with London's Royal Court Theatre.

As we prepare to celebrate European Capital of Culture in 2008, the Theatres have a variety of exciting projects in development which grow on the foundations of recent work.

"A stunning theatrical coup." (Liverpool Echo on *Unprotected*)

Around the main production programme, the theatres run a range of projects and activities to create opportunities and endeavour to support writers at every career stage. The commissioning programme invests in the creation of new work for both the Everyman and Playhouse stages.

The Young Writer's Programme is a year-long programme working alongside experienced practitioners, which nurtures and develops exciting new voices to create a new generation of Liverpool writers. An annual new writing festival, Everyword, offers a busy and popular week of seminars, sofa talks and work-in-progress readings.

"A rare play that captures the essence of Liverpool and its people without plunging into the usual clichés." (Liverpool Daily Post on *Paradise Bound*)

For more information about the Everyman and Playhouse - including the full programme, off-stage activities such as Playwright Support, and ways in which you can support our investment in talent - visit www.everymanplayhouse.com

Credits

Cast (in alphabetical order)

Michael Donohue	**Mark Arends**
Eileen McGrath/Liliane	**Alisa Arnah**
Theresa Donohue	**Leanne Best**
Colin/Docker	**Paul Duckworth**
Father Quiggan/Mickey	**Denis Quilligan**
Vinnie Phelan	**Niall Refoy**
J J Collins	**Michael Ryan**
Angela Donohue/Veronica	**Cathy Tyson**

Company

Writer	**Stephen Sharkey**
Director	**Serdar Bilis**
Designer	**Colin Richmond**
Music and Sound Designer	**Dan Jones**
Lighting Designer	**Ian Scott**
Movement Director	**Scott Graham** for Frantic Assembly
Costume Supervisor	**Marie Jones**
Assistant Director	**Adam Cross**
Casting Director	**Ginny Schiller**
Production Manager	**Emma Wright**
Stage Manager	**Sarah Lewis**
Deputy Stage Manager	**Roxanne Vella**
Assistant Stage Manager	**Helen Wilson**
Wardrobe Mistress	**Tracey Thompson**
Lighting Operators	**Andy Webster**
	Dave Sherman
Sound Engineer	**Marc Williams**
Stage Crew	**Howard Macaulay**

Cast

Mark Arends
Michael Donohue

Mark trained at LAMDA.

Mark's theatre credits include:
Urban Legend (Liverpool Everyman); *Vieux Carré* (Library Theatre, Manchester); *What Every Woman Knows* (Royal Exchange, Manchester); *The UN Inspector* and *A Dream Play* (National Theatre); *Fierce* (Assembly Rooms, Edinburgh and tour); *Dealing* (Upstart Theatre Company) and *Tamburlaine The Great* (Rose Theatre, Southwark).

Television credits include: *The Bill, The Innocence Project, Silent Witness, Casualty* and *Holby City.*

Film credits include: *Pride and Prejudice* and *Mother and Son.*

Radio credits include: *Born For War.*

Alisa Arnah
Eileen McGrath/Liliane

Alisa trained at RADA, graduating in 2005. Productions there included *The Fool, On The Razzle, The Knight of The Burning Pestle* and *A Chorus of Disapproval.*

Alisa's theatre credits include:
A Woman of No Importance (Salisbury Theatre); *Harvey* (Manchester Royal Exchange); *House and Garden* (Harrogate Theatre) and *Riders to The Sea* and *Shadows of The Glen* (Southwark Playhouse).

Television includes: *Jane Eyre.*

Film includes: *How To Be* and *Dancing With Lucy.*

Cast

Leanne Best
Theresa Donohue

Leanne's theatre credits include:
Unprotected (Traverse Theatre,
Edinburgh); *34* (Fecund Theatre
Company); *The Way Home,
Macbeth, The Morris* and
Unprotected (Liverpool Everyman);
Solitary Confinement (King's Head
Theatre) and *Our Country's Good,
The Flint Street Nativity* and
Popcorn (Liverpool Playhouse).

Television credits include:
*Casualty, Heatwave, Wire in the
Blood, Memory of Water, Casbah -
A Documentary, New Street Law*
and *Mobile.*

Radio credits include: *The
Importance of Being Earnest* and
Hen Night.

Film credits includes: *Choices.*

Paul Duckworth
Colin/Docker

Paul's theatre credits include:
Unprotected (Liverpool Everyman
and Traverse, Edinburgh); *Urban
Legend* (Liverpool Everyman); *You
Are Here* (Unity Theatre); *Golden
Boy, Man Who Stole a Winter Coat*
and *The Corrupted Angel* (Base
Chorus Company); *Slappers and
Slapheads* (Tour); *River Fever*
(Unity Theatre); *Moving Voices*
(Sheffield Crucible); *The Man Who
Cracked, Backwater* (National tour -
Spike Theatre Company), *Madam
I'm Adam* (Edinburgh Festival 2005
- Spike Theatre Company) , *The
True Tales of Baron Munchausen*
(Outdoor performance - Spike
Theatre Company) and *Hoof,* an
improvisation group made up of
Rejects Revenge and Spike Theatre
companies.

Television credits include:
Brookside, The Courtroom and
Mobile.

Film credits include: *Backbeat.*

Radio credits include: *Tin Man.*

Denis Quilligan
Father Quiggan/Mickey

Denis's theatre credits include:
Frobishers Gold (The Shaw Theatre
and Menagerie Theatre); *Frongoch*
(North Wales Stage Company);
Philadelphia Here I Come (Gaiety
Dublin, Liverpool Playhouse and
tour); *Playboy of The Western
World* (Manchester Royal
Exchange); *Juno & The Paycock* and
Playboy of The Western World
(Citizens Theatre and The Arches,
Glasgow); *The Birthday Party*
(Library Theatre, Manchester); *Juno
& The Paycock, Dancing at
Lughnasa* and *Life of Wolfe Tone*
(Royal Lyceum, Edinburgh) and
*Wexford Trilogy: Poor Beast In The
Rain* (Bush Theatre).

Television credits include: *The
Man Who Lost Ireland, The Baby
War, The Key, The Bill* and *Father
Ted.*

Film credits include: *Conspiracy of
Silence* and *The Projectionist.*

Niall Refoy
Vinnie Phelan

Niall's theatre credits include:
Uncle Vanya and *Macbeth*
(Harrogate Theatre); *All's Well
That Ends Well, Coriolanus,
Barbarians* and *Pericles* (Royal
Shakespeare Company); *Dead
Guilty* (Bill Kenwright Productions)
and *The Flag* (Moving Theatre).

Television includes: *Pieces of a
Silver Lining, Lewis, The Ghost
Squad, Last Rights, Casualty,
Rosemary and Thyme, Rose &
Maloney, Vice, Holby City, Bugs,
The Vanishing Man, The Round
Tower, The Bill, Dangerfield, Ain't
Misbehavin', Thieftakers, Between
The Lines, The Bill, Soldier, Soldier,
Tuesday, Virtual Murder, Eastenders*
and *Grey Clay Dolls.*

Film includes: *Exorcist: The
Beginning, Neighbours, Spartacus*
and *Two Deaths.*

Cast

Michael Ryan
J J Collins

Michael's theatre credits include: *Paradise Bound* (Liverpool Everyman); *The Doll Tower* and *The Trial* (Unity Theatre, Liverpool); *Play Your Cards Right* (Various London Theatres); *Pause For Thought* (Mermaid Theatre, London); *Road* and *Hay Fever* (Neptune Theatre, Liverpool); *Liz Lockhead's Dracula* (Everyman Theatre, Liverpool) and *The Longest Night Alone* (Green House/Philharmonic Hall, Liverpool).

Television credits include: *Dream Team*, *Dockers* and *Innocent Party*.

Film credits include: *Revengers Tragedy*, *In His Life* (John Lennon biopic), *Across The Universe*, *Contenders* and *The Landlord*.

Radio credits include: *Hush Little Baby*.

Cathy Tyson
Angela Donohue/Veronica

Cathy's theatre credits include: *The Liverpool Blitz Show*, *The Tempest* and *Hamlet* (Liverpool Everyman); *Golden Girls*, *Mephisto* and *Red Noses* (Royal Shakespeare Company); *Educating Rita* and *Pygmalion* (Theatr Clwyd); *The Taming of The Shrew* (Regent's Park Open Air Theatre); *Anthony and Cleopatra* and *As You Like It* (English Shakespeare Company); *The Merchant of Venice* (Birmingham Rep) and *Mum's The Word* (Alberry Theatre, West End).

Television credits include: *Bonkers*, *Grange Hill*, *Lewis*, *Stand By Your Man*, *Night and Day*, *Always and Everyone*, *Band of Gold*, *Angels*, *Rules of Engagement*, *The Lenny Henry Show*, *Scully*, *The Bill* and *Holby City*.

Film credits include: *The Old Man Who Read Love Stories*, *The Golden Years*, *Turbulence*, *The Serpent and The Rainbow*, *Mona Lisa*, *Priest*, *Killing Time* and *Body*.

Company

Stephen Sharkey
Writer

Stephen has just completed a year as one of 'The 50', a Royal Court/BBC new writing initiative.

Stephen's theatre credits include: *Ion* (The Gate); *The Glass Slipper* and *The Old Curiosity Shop* (Southwark Playhouse); *Oblomov, The Gambler* and *Tomorrow Is A Lovely Day* (Pleasance, Edinburgh).

Radio credits include: *All Of You On The Good Earth* which won the 2004 Society of Authors Imison Award, *The Visitation* and the forthcoming *Kepler's Mum's A Witch* for Radio 4 this Christmas.

Forthcoming work includes a new version of *A Christmas Carol* for Northern Stage in Newcastle and a musical for children based on *Birds* by Aristophanes. He curates The Miniaturists, a regular night of short plays at the Arcola Theatre in London, which will be coming to the Everyman on June 6th as part of Everyword.

Serdar Bilis
Director

Serdar is a part time Associate Director at the Liverpool Everyman and Playhouse and the Arcola Theatre in London.

He is from Istanbul where he trained as an actor before completing a directing course at Middlesex University and the Royal National Theatre.

Serdar's directing credits include: *A Family Affair* by Ostrovsky, *Tartuffe* by Molière and *Night Just Before the Forests* by Bernard Marie Koltès all at the Arcola.

Company

Colin Richmond
Designer

Colin trained at the Royal Welsh College of Music and Drama gaining a 1st Class BA Hons in Theatre Design. He was a 2003 Linbury Prize for Theatre Design finalist and a Resident Designer as part of the Royal Shakespeare Company's Trainee Programme 2004-2005. He is also a 2007 2D-3D design exhibitionist with the Society of British Theatre Designers in Nottingham.

Design credits include: *L'Opera Seria* (Batignano Opera Festival, Tuscany); *Human Rites* (Southwark Playhouse); *Hansel and Gretel* (Northampton Theatre Royal); *Lowdat* and *The Bolt Hole* (Birmingham Rep); *Play/Not I* (Battersea Arts Centre, winner JMK young directors award); *Twelfth Night* and *Bad Girls - The Musical* (West Yorkshire Playhouse); *Breakfast with Mugabe* (Royal Shakespeare Company); *House of The Gods* (Music Theatre Wales, Linbury, National tour); *Restoration* (Oxford Stage Company, Headlong, Bristol Old Vic); *Shadow of a Gunman* (Glasgow Citizen's Theatre); *Hansel and Gretel* (Dundee Rep), *Europe* (Dundee Rep, Barbican) and *Suddenly Last Summer* (Clwyd Theatr Cymru).

Television includes: Assistant Production Designer (set) for *Doctor Who* (series one).

Dan Jones
Music and Sound Designer

Dan read music at the University of Oxford, studied contemporary music theatre at the Banff Centre for the Arts and studied electro-acoustic composition and programming at the Centro Ricerche Musicali in Rome.

Dan's recent theatre credits include: *A Midsummer Night's Dream* (Dundee Rep), *So Long Life* (Bath Theatre Royal and tour) and *Betrayal* (Northcott, Exeter).

Television credits include: *The Life of Mammals, Strange, Twockers, Tomorrow La Scala* and *The Spectre of Hope.*

Film credits include: *Shadow of the Vampire* and *Max*, for which he received the 2004 Ivor Novello Award for Best Film Score.

Dan is also the co-creator of *Sky Orchestra*, where music is played from seven hot air balloons positioned over a city, making it one of the largest sound works in the world. His music has also been used by the Rambert Dance Company, The European Space Agency and was incorporated in *Paradise Omeros* which is exhibited at Tate Modern, London.

He is a founder member and co-artistic director of Sound and Fury Theatre Company whose productions pioneer the immersive use of experimental sound design.

Ian Scott
Lighting Designer

Recent theatre credits: *Futurology* (Suspect Culture); *Europe* (Barbican BITE and Dundee Rep); *The 39 Steps* (Criterion Theatre); *Flat Stanley* (West Yorkshire Playhouse); *Blasted* (Graeae); *The Wedding Dance* (Nitro); *Dysfunction* (Soho Theatre); *Sinner* (Stan Won't Dance) and *Child of the Divide* (Tamasha and Polka Theatre).

Other credits include: *Longitude* (Greenwich Theatre); *Timeless* (Suspect Culture); *Oh What a Lovely War* (National Theatre); *Observe the Sons of Ulster Marching Towards the Somme* (Abbey Theatre); *Slamdunk* (Nitro); *Map of the Heart* (Salisbury Playhouse); *Knots* (CoisCeim Dance Theatre); *Blown* (Theatre Royal, Plymouth); *Unheimlich Spine* (David Glass Ensemble); *Shadow of a Gunman* (Lyric Theatre, Belfast); *Peeling* (Graeae); *Frogs* (Nottingham Playhouse); *Caledonia Dreaming* (7:84); *Taylor's Dummies* (Gecko); *Two Step* (Push @ Almeida); *Henry IV - Part 1* (Peacock Theatre, Dublin); *Crazy Horse* (Paines Plough) and *Stalinland* (Citizens Theatre).

Ian is an Associate Artist of Suspect Culture and a regular collaborator with the pioneering theatre company, Graeae.

Scott Graham
Movement Director

Scott is the Artistic Director and co-founder of Frantic Assembly.

His director/performer credits for the company include: *Hymns, On Blindness, Tiny Dynamite, Heavenly, Sell Out, Zero, Flesh, Klub* and *Look Back in Anger*. He has also co-directed *pool (no water), Dirty Wonderland, Rabbit, Peepshow* and *Underworld* for the company.

Scott's other directing credits include: *Home* (National Theatre of Scotland) and *It's A Long Road* (Polka Theatre).

Choreography and movement director credits include: *Market Boy* (National Theatre); *Villette* (Stephen Joseph Theatre); *Vs* (Karim Tonsi Dance Company, Cairo); *Improper* (Bare Bones Dance Company); *Dazzling Medusa* and *A Bear Called Paddington* (Polka Theatre) and *Stuart Little* (Ambassadors Theatre Group).

Company

Marie Jones
Costume Supervisor

Marie studied fashion and then moved on to Theatre Costume Interpretation at Mable Fletcher College. Marie's work as a freelance costumier has included costumes for Oldham Coliseum, The Royal Exchange, West Yorkshire Playhouse, Jimmy McGovern's film *Liam*, *Beyond Friendship* for Mersey Television and the creation of many panto dames who have appeared on the Everyman stage.

She has worked extensively at the Everyman and Playhouse and has recently been employed full time as resident Wardrobe Supervisor. Most recently Marie's work here includes: *Much Ado About Nothing, The Electric Hills, The Flint Street Nativity, The Tempest, Unprotected, Billy Liar, Who's Afraid of Virginia Woolf?, Urban Legend, Fly, Breezeblock Park, The Entertainer, Still Life and The Astonished Heart, Ma Rainey's Black Bottom* and *The Anniversary*.

Marie's other credits include: *Brick Up the Mersey Tunnels* at The Royal Court, Brouhaha International Street Festival, *Working Class Hero* on the recent *Imagine* DVD, Costume Supervisor for many shows at LIPA, The Splash Project, for MYPT, and *Twopence to Cross The Mersey* at the Liverpool Empire.

Adam Cross
Assistant Director

Adam was born in Liverpool and has studied at the University of York, King's College London and RADA.

He was attached to the Everyman and Playhouse in 2006 through the LEADS young director programme and is delighted to return. Recent production elsewhere include *Hedda Gabler* and *Endgame*. He also sits on the script reading panel for Soho Theatre and Writers' Centre.

Ginny Schiller
Casting Director

Ginny's theatre credits include:
All My Sons (Liverpool Playhouse);
The Canterbury Tales and the
Complete Works Festival (Royal
Shakespeare Company); *Imagine
This* (Theatre Royal, Plymouth);
Dancing at Lughnasa (Lyric
Theatre, Belfast); *Macbeth* and *How
Many Miles to Basra?* (West
Yorkshire Playhouse); *The Taming
of the Shrew* (Wilton's Music Hall);
*French without Tears, Someone Else's
Shoes, Mother Courage, The Old
Country, Hamlet, Rosencrantz and
Guildenstern are Dead* and *Twelfth
Night* (all as Casting Associate for
English Touring Theatre);
Dr Faustus and *The Taming of the
Shrew* (Bristol Old Vic); *A Passage
to India* (Shared Experience);
When the World Was Green (Young
Vic); *Amadeus* (CLSO); *Macbeth*
(Albery) and extensive work at Soho
Theatre, Chichester Festival
Theatre for the Royal Shakespeare
Company.

Television and film credits include:
*The Kingdom, Notes on a Scandal,
George Orwell - A Life in Pictures*
(Emmy Award Winner), *The Bill*
and *The Falklands Play*.

Radio credits include: *Felix Holt
the Radical, The Pickwick Papers,
Tender is the Night* and *The Bride's
Chamber*.

The company wishes to thank:

Cains for their support of Everyman
and Playhouse press nights; Sydney
Jones Library, University of
Liverpool and Ged at the Everyman.

Staff

Leah Abbott Box Office Assistant, Vicky Adlard Administrator, Laura Arends Marketing Campaigns Manager, Deborah Aydon Executive Director, Jane Baxter Box Office Manager, Rob Beamer Chief Electrician (Playhouse), Lindsey Bell Technician, Suzanne Bell Literary Manager, Serdar Bilis Associate Director, Gemma Bodinetz Artistic Director, Emma Callan Cleaning Staff, Moira Callaghan Theatre and Community Administrator, Colin Carey Security Officer, Joe Cornmell Finance Assistant, Stephen Dickson Finance Assistant, Angela Dooley Cleaning Staff, Alison Eley Finance Assistant, Roy Francis Maintenance Technician, Rosalind Gordon Deputy Box Office Manager, Carl Graceffa Bar Supervisor, Mike Gray Deputy Technical Stage Manager, Helen Grey Stage Door Receptionist, Helen Griffiths House Manager, Jayne Gross Development Manager, Lesley Hallam Stage Door Receptionist, Talib Hamafaraj Box Office Assistant, Poppy Harrison Box Office Assistant, Stuart Holden IT and Communications Manager, David Jordan Fire Officer, Sarah Kelly Assistant House Manager, Sue Kelly Cleaning Staff, Steven Kennett Assistant Maintenance Technician (Performance), Sven Key Fire Officer, Lynn-Marie Kilgallon Internal Courier, Andrew King Stage Door Receptionist, Gavin Lamb Marketing Communications Officer, Rachel Littlewood Community Outreach Co-ordinator, Robert Longthorne Building Development Director, Howard Macaulay Deputy Chief Technician (Stage), Ged Manson Cleaning Staff, Christine Mathews-Sheen Director of Finance and Administration, Peter McKenna Cleaning Staff, Jason McQuaide Technical Stage Manager (Playhouse), Kirstin Mead Development Officer, Dan Meigh Youth Theatre Director, Liz Nolan Assistant to the Directors, Lizzie Nunnery Literary Assistant, Vivian O'Callaghan Youth Theatre Administrator, Sarah Ogle Marketing Director, Sean Pritchard Senior Production Manager, Collette Rawlinson Stage Door Receptionist, Victoria Rope Programme Co-ordinator, Rebecca Ross-Williams Theatre and Community Director, Jeff Salmon Technical Director, Hayley Sephton House Manager, Steve Sheridan Assistant Maintenance Technician, David Sherman Deputy Chief Technician (Electrics), Jackie Skinner Education Co-ordinator, Louise Sutton Box Office Supervisor, Jennifer Tallon-Cahill Deputy Chief Electrician, Matthew Taylor Marketing and Press Assistant, Pippa Taylor Press and Media Officer, Marie Thompson Cleaning Supervisor/Receptionist, Scott Turner Market Planning Manager, Hellen Turton Security Officer, Paul Turton Finance Manager, Andrew Webster Lighting Technician, Marc Williams Chief Technician (Everyman), Emma Wright Production Manager.

Thanks to all our Front of House team and casual Box Office staff.

Board Members:
Cllr Warren Bradley, Professor Michael Brown (Chair), Mike Carran, Michelle Charters, Rod Holmes, Vince Killen, Professor E. Rex Makin, Andrew Moss, Roger Phillips, Sara Williams, Ivan Wadeson.

The regulations of Liverpool City Council provide that:
The public may leave at the end of the performance by all exit doors and all exit doors must at that time be open. Note: all Liverpool theatres can be emptied in three minutes or less if the audience leaves in an orderly manner. All gangways, passages, staircases and exits must be kept entirely free from obstruction. Persons shall not be permitted to stand or sit in any of the intersecting gangways or stand in any unseated space in the auditorium unless standing in such space has been authorised by the City Council.

SMOKING AND DRINKING GLASSES ARE NOT ALLOWED IN THE AUDITORIUM AT ANY TIME.

We would like to remind you that the bleep of digital watches, pagers and mobile phones during the performance may distract the actors and your fellow audience members. Please ensure they are switched off for the duration of the performance. You are strongly advised not to leave bags and other personal belongings unattended anywhere in the theatre.

For my father, Bernard

Acknowledgements

No writer's an island. To all at the Everyman, especially Serdar, Suzanne, Gemma and Deborah, I'm sensible of the honour.

Playwrights Vanessa Bates, Samantha Ellis and Rebecca Nesvet gave advice, and the Monsterists were an inspiration. Ellen Hughes directed a reading of *The May Queen* and sharpened it, as did the very bright group of actors who workshopped the story at the Playhouse during a punishing heatwave last summer. My agent Micheline has kept me on my toes. As ever, my wife Rebecca was the play's first reader, editor and critic.

I'm indebted to many sources, among them *Alone of All Her Sex*, Marina Warner's study of the Virgin Mary, *An Underworld at War* by Donald Thomas, and Beryl Wade's brilliant memoir of wartime in Liverpool, *Storm over the Mersey*.

The May Queen

Characters

Theresa Donohue
Angela Donohue, *her mother*
Michael Donohue, *her brother*
Vinnie Phelan, *Angela's lover*
Eileen McGrath, *Angela's friend*
JJ Collins, *Michael's friend*
Liliane, *a Jewish German refugee*
Colin, *Vinnie's sidekick*
Father Quiggan, *a priest*
Docker
Mickey, *a gravedigger*
Veronica

Setting

Liverpool, during the May Blitz, 1941.

A Small Note On Punctuation

Some lines are written as questions but do not end with a
question mark – e.g. 'What's the news then, Jack.' This is to
encourage the line to be read with a 'down beat' at the end.

Scene One

Catholic church, very early morning.

Theresa *comes and kneels before a statue of the Virgin. She has a satchel, and she's carrying a chain of wild flowers.*

As she sings, without enthusiasm, she drops the flowers at the statue's feet, one by one.

Theresa
Bring flowers of the rarest
Bring blossoms the fairest
From garden and woodland and hillside and dale
Our full hearts are swelling
Our glad voices telling
The praise of the loveliest flower of the vale

O Mary we crown thee with blossoms today
Queen of the Angels and Queen of the May

Their lady they name thee
Their mistress proclaim thee
O grant that thy children on earth be as true
As long as the bowers
Are radiant with flowers
As long as the azure shall keep its bright hue

O Mary we crown thee with blossoms today
Queen of the Angels and Queen of the May.

She takes off the satchel and pours out the contents – pieces of stone and dust. During the following we become aware that unbeknown to **Theresa**, **Father Quiggan** *is watching her.*

Theresa   Satisfied, are yer. Me dad's gravestone, what's left of it. It said, 'In loving memory, Francis Edward Donohue, killed by enemy action'. But that's a load o' crap, as you well know.

Or did you miss it when he was brained to death? Lookin' the wrong way, were yer, when Phelan's lackeys carted his body to the docks? I know every'n cos I've heard them, haven't I.

Pillow talk. After they've done the beast with two backs. And me dad, well, he's just one of thousands, isn't he, easy to miss. There goes his grave, coffin, body and all, smashed to pieces by a stray bomb. But so what, ey, he was dead anyway. And them that put him there – Phelan and me mam – they gonna get off with five Hail Marys and five Our Fathers, is that it? That what yer sayin'? What exactly *is* it yer sayin', Queen of the May? All part of some big plan, is it? Or what? Could you not just TELL ME? Could you not just SAY SOMETHING?

I'm down on me knees every night prayin' for our Michael to come back. Every bleedin' night for six months. Like talking to a brick wall, isn't it, let's be honest –

Bring him home. Then . . . Then I'll throw a veil over you, so you won't have to look. It'll be like the Easter vigil, won't it. And when the dust's settled, when it's done, I'll come and make me confession to yer, alright? – 'Mary Immaculate, forgive me, forgive our Michael, we're awful sorry.' And then I'll say me rosaries and me acts of contrition, many as yer want, and we'll all live happy ever after. Cos it's just words, isn't it, girl? As long as we say the words we'll be alright . . .

Hail Mary, full of grace
The Lord is with thee –
Blessed art thou among women,
Blessed is the fruit of thy womb –

She stops, backs away.

D'yer know what? I used to love you so much –

She exits.

Father Quiggan *enters. He's carrying a broom, which he uses to sweep away the pieces of stone and dust.*

Father Quiggan Hail, Holy Mother, Queen of Heaven and the Dead. Here I am. Still in one piece! For the time being anyway. More than can be said for poor Frank.

I'm your temple-sweeper now, look. Why should only the pagan goddesses have a temple-sweeper and not yourself?

I pity the child. I know her of old. There is a shadow on her heart, grows darker by the day.

And if Michael comes – if Michael comes.

Only let her glimpse the chasm, won't you. Let her see the deep and the dark of it. But let her not fall into it, now. Let her not fall.

He genuflects before the statue, then exits.

Scene Two

The docks, Liverpool.

Enter **Michael** *and* **John Joe**. *Dishevelled, dressed in shabby dark clothes.*

There's an air raid in progress.

Michael *is distracted.* **JJ** *nervous.*

JJ   Michael – was crawlin' with redcaps back there, if yer 'adn't noticed. Can't be stoppin' too long, Michael.

Michael (*scanning the devastation*)   Look at that. Jesus Christ.

JJ   Yeah, well. There's a war on, yer know.

Michael   Fires. Hundreds o' them. Far as yer can see.

JJ   They're havin' a proper go, aren't they?

Michael   State of that dock – the Huskisson.

JJ   I know, yeah –

Michael   Me dad used to take us down there to see the liners comin' in from America, all the White Star ships, y'know – the *Majestic*, the *Ceramic* –

JJ   We should vamoose.

Michael   The tall tales he told us.

JJ   Am I talkin' to meself 'ere or what.

Michael (*taking out cigarettes for them both*)   We're alright 'ere for a minute.

JJ   Think so, do yer.

They light up.

What's that stink, anyway? Horrible burny stink, that is. Like Simon's hair when we found him, d'yer remember? God, he stunk.

A distant boom.

Aye aye.

Then a somewhat nearer one . . .

Talk about outta the fryin' pan –

Michael   We're going straight to hell when we go, yer know that. Think they'll be waitin' for us?

JJ   Who?

Michael   Ones we killed.

JJ   Christ. Don't.

Michael   That one in About Turn. He'll be there.

JJ   Aye. Well. All the more reason to stay alive, isn't it.

Pause.

Michael   We get caught, they'll break yer neck for yer.

JJ   I know that, don't I.

Michael   No one's gonna blame yer if yer give it a miss.

JJ   No chance.

Michael   Good.

JJ   God only knows what state your Theresa'll be in.

Michael   Soon see.

JJ   Under the same roof as the bastard.

Pause.

Remember the night we left? Yer arl fella singin' 'The Dyin' Rebel' –

Michael   For a change.

JJ   Always goin' on at us to join the IRA –

Michael   'If yer want somethin' worth fightin' for, lad . . . ' And Danny Riordan'd have us in his brigade at the drop of a hat.

JJ   Stupid Irish get.

Michael   Himself there at the bar, laughin' and jokin' with me mam. Now he's fuckin' sleepin' with her, in me dad's bed? Don't even wanna call her me mam any more, God forgive me –

A well-oiled **Docker** *is passing by, trailing his coat (i.e. looking for a scrap).*

JJ   Aye aye –

Docker   Ey! Ey, *you* – 'oo yer lookin' at?

JJ   Nah, yer alright, mate, walk on.

Docker   Walk on?

JJ   What I said.

Docker   Is it now? And *'oo* the *fuck* are *you*, to call *me* yer mate?

JJ   JJ Collins, painter and decorator, at yer service.

Michael *gets up, wearily*

Docker *(rolling his sleeves up)*   Decorator, that right? Yer won't be able to hang wallpaper very well with yer fuckin' ribs broke, will yer, JJ, ey?

JJ   Yer alright, Michael –

Docker   Who's this, yer boyfriend? You wan' a go n' all, do yer – ?

Michael *puts his hand in his jacket, draws a pistol and readies it.*

Docker   WHOA! – What yer playin' at, lad? – Bloody hell –

Michael   Asked yer to walk on, didn't he?

JJ *(anxiously looking about)*   Redcaps, Michael.

Michael *menaces the* **Docker***, his temper roused.*

Michael   Didn't he!

Docker   Aye, yeah, he did, right enough – Just fancied a ruck, didn't I – Don't shoot me, will yer – ?

Michael *lands a blow with the butt of the pistol. The* **Docker** *cowers.*

Docker   I've got a wife an' kids –

Michael   Oh aye? 'Ow d'yer manage that?

JJ   Michael. Easy.

Michael   Sit down. I *said* –

Docker *sits.*

JJ *sits down, gives the* **Docker** *a cigarette.*

JJ   'Ere y'are.

Michael   What d'yer say?

Docker   Thanks. Thank you.

JJ   What's the news then, Jack?

Docker   What about?

JJ   You bein' funny? Middle of a world war, aren't we. Whaddya know, whaddya say.

Docker   Well, yers've picked a fine time, alright –

Michael   Thinks we've deserted – don't yer – ?

Docker   I wouldn't mind! Honest to God, wouldn't blame yers – got brains in yer heads.

Michael   Been keeping yours down, 'ave yer, mate?

Docker   Docker, aren't I – reserve occupation –

Michael   Oh aye.

JJ   Wha've yer been up to then, Jack. Been doin' yer bit?

Docker   Aye, yeah – unloadin' the convoys from America and all that.

Michael   How many scams yer been workin'?

Docker   What scams?

More menacing from **Michael***. He slaps the* **Docker** *around the head.*

JJ (*to* **Michael**)   Knock it off, will yer. (*To* **Docker**.) So, where've yer got yerself bladdered then?

Docker   Oh, yer know, just some dive in Lime Street – I'm normally in the the Eagle on Balliol Road there, but it's took a whippin' Friday night. Forty dead.

JJ   Yer jokin'.

Docker   The things that go on, tellin' yer.

JJ   Like what? Come 'ead, we could do with a laugh.

Docker   Like Tuesday – this ship just pulled in from New Zealand, the *Bluebell*, just sittin' there in the Gladstone, chocker with lamb and mutton – took about five direct. Burned all night and all next day.

JJ   That's it. The smell.

Michael   Aye, yeah – roast meat –

Docker   There was boilin' fat runnin' in the gutters. These women come flyin' down from Scottie Road with pots and pans tryna catch it.

JJ   Yer turn yer back for five minutes . . . Off yer go now.

Docker   Ey?

JJ   Sling it.

Michael   Scram.

Docker   But I was just gettin' warmed up –

Michael *goes for him and the* **Docker** *starts to run away.* **Michael** *gives him a hefty kick up the backside. Exit* **Docker**.

JJ   Let's get out of 'ere.

Air-raid warning begins, crackle of anti-aircraft guns.

Michael   Ack-ack.

They begin to go.

JJ   Who *was* Gladstone, anyway?

Michael   A big noise on the railway, way back when. Picked a fight with a runaway engine.

JJ   That was Huskisson, wasn't it.

Michael   Oh aye, yeah.

Exit **Michael** *and* **JJ**.

Scene Three

At the **Donohues'**.

Angela *is comforting newly-widowed* **Eileen**, *a neighbour. She is heavily pregnant with her first.* **Theresa** *sits apart.*

Angela   Come on, hon.

Eileen   I'm a right mess.

Angela   Don't be soft.

Theresa   Don't be sorry, Eileen.

Eileen   I promised meself, y'know, if the worst came –

She breaks down again.

Angela   'S alright, hon.

Eileen   Must bring it all back for yer –

Angela   I never forget for a minute. Course I don't. But time's a healer, as they say. Changes how you think of it.

Eileen   How d'yer mean?

Angela   It's like it happened to a different you, somewhere else.

Theresa   Oh aye.

Angela   Did they say how it happened?

Eileen   Only the ship got separated from the convoy, and that was it.

Angela   Mother o' God.

Eileen   Three weeks ago it happened. There were fourteen survivors.

Angela   Go 'way.

Eileen   An American ship picked them up. Most of them were from the kitchens, it said.

Theresa   I'm sorry your Peter wasn't one of them.

Eileen (*breaking down as she says this*)   They got taken to Florida. That's how the navy know all the details –

Angela   Arr, come here, love.

She holds **Eileen** *while she cries.*

Eileen   He would've been such a good dad –

Angela   I know, sweetheart.

Eileen   Every time it kicks –

Angela   Looks like a boy, to me.

Eileen   D'yer think?

Angela   Big enough!

Theresa   Old wives' tale, that –

Eileen   As long as it's healthy.

Angela   And good-lookin'!

Eileen   Girl or boy, I don't mind.

Angela   If it's a boy I bet he's the spit of Peter.

Eileen   Yer reckon?

Angela   Bound to be.

Eileen   I'll still have something left.

Angela   Course you will, sweetheart.

Theresa   What have you thought about names?

Eileen   Oh – I was gonna ask him when he got back –

Angela   I like George. And Christopher. If I'd had another
boy –

Theresa   I like Francis. Like me dad.

Eileen   God love him.

Angela   Amen.

Eileen   Michael's nice. Oh, I shouldn't – sorry.

Angela   Why, wha've yer done?

Eileen   Don't want to upset you.

Angela   I always loved that name. Ever since I was a girl.

Eileen   Were yer sweet on one?

Angela   Could say that. I was the May Queen once upon a
time –

Eileen   Were yer?

Angela   Before the first war, never mind this one.

Eileen   Oh, I never forgave Catty O'Brien. She was Queen
in my year.

Angela   *She* was in *hers*, weren't yer.

Eileen   That's right –

Theresa   Don't remember.

Angela   Yes, you do.

Eileen   Your dress was absolutely gorgeous.

Angela   Me and our Val made that. It was comical – we robbed me mam's net curtains for a veil.

Theresa   They made me sneeze non-stop.

Angela   She had a cob on with us for days.

Theresa   You could've washed them first.

Angela   Made a show of me.

Theresa   Worst thing was, Eil, Father Quiggan gave me his hanky, and when I opened it there was a big bogey –

Angela   She had one of her tantrums.

Theresa   I nearly threw up.

Angela   When I was Queen, the SVP presented me with this book, *The Lives of the Saints*. And there was this picture of the Archangel Michael, wasn't there. He was fightin' this horrible monster, could've been the Devil himself, I was never sure. But I couldn't get past it, he just looked so fantastic there in all his armour, standin' over this evil thing with the red eyes that he's stabbed right through with his what-d'yer-call-it, his spear. And this look on his face, like he's just tidyin' up some mess. Serene doesn't cover it. Well. Didn't I take this book everywhere I bleedin' went.

Eileen   I pray for your Michael every night. To see him in this house again.

Angela   All of us do, love.

Eileen   I can't believe there's been no word.

Angela   Far as I'm concerned, until they bring me his ashes –

Theresa   Oh, 'ere we go –

Angela   Till someone stands here hand on heart and swears to me he's not, far as I'm concerned he's out there somewhere, alive and well. They can keep their yellow envelopes. Men go missin' all the time.

Eileen   Billy Mangan.

Angela   Billy Mangan. He said they all just legged it after Dunkirk, they just said, sod this, I'm off –

Eileen   Sod this for a game o' soldiers!

Angela   Face the music some other time. I reckon our Michael's keepin' his head down till the dust settles. Then he'll come home. When he's ready.

Theresa   When he's ready?

Angela   What I said.

Theresa   He's not comin' back, Ma.

Angela   Here she is with the pessimism.

Theresa   Soon as he got the letter –

Angela   The post's a bloody shambles, yer know that –

Theresa   He'd've come flyin' the minute he found out –

Angela   What did I just say?

Theresa   As if you want him back.

Angela   Yer what? He's me son, isn't he?

Theresa   He hates Phelan's guts.

Angela   Oh, for God's sake –

Theresa   He always has.

Angela   I don't know why.

Theresa   What'd be the first thing he'd do if he came through that door?

Angela   Knock it off, will yer?

Theresa   Lucky for you he's not going to.

Angela   How can you say that?

Theresa   Dunkirk was nearly a year ago, Mother. Do I have to spell it out for yer? He's *dead*.

Angela   Oh, that's nice. Think of Eileen, will yer –

Eileen   I'm alright –

Angela   Until they put his ashes in my hands – that's all I'm sayin'.

Theresa   You're fuckin' unbelievable, you are.

Angela   Ey! D'you know what your problem is, girl? You've no hope in yer. Yer wouldn't know a silver lining if it pissed in yer tea.

Theresa   The silver lining. Yeah. 'Ere y'are, Eileen, what d'yer reckon – if I give yer a shoebox full of money, will yer stop crying for your husband?

Angela   You little cow –

Theresa   This one did.

Angela   Don't listen, Eileen.

Theresa   My mother did.

Angela   I'll swing for you, girl, if you don't take that back –

Theresa   Oh, you'll swing alright.

Angela   You've got one sick little mind –

Theresa   Sick? I'll tell yer what's sick – Phelan shackin' up with yer!

Angela   She's got a vicious streak in her, this one.

Theresa   Wonder where from.

Angela   I'll brain you in a minute –

Pause.

Theresa   When were you last at confession, Mother?

Angela   Watch it, girl.

Theresa   I'm only askin'.

Angela   And I'm tellin yer.

Theresa   I'd like to've been a fly on that wall.

Angela   That's enough –

Theresa   Or what?

Angela   Your mouth wants washin' out –

Theresa   Does it.

Angela   And I'm the one to do it for yer –

Theresa   Are yer now.

Eileen   Ange –

Theresa   It's just words, Ma.

Angela   Yeah, an' I'll take them words and ram them down yer friggin' throat, yer cheeky little harpie, yer –

Eileen   She doesn't mean nothing, do yer, Theresa –

Theresa   Oh don't I? Don't I mean nothing? One of these days, Mother. One of these days. You and yer fuckin' sugar daddy.

She exits with a door slam.

Angela   I'm awful sorry, Eileen.

Eileen   It's alright.

Angela   The things she comes out with, I swear –

Eileen *winces as her baby kicks.*

Angela   Kickin' off, is he?

Eileen   Yeah –

Angela   Not surprised with all the shoutin' and bawlin'.

Eileen   A lot on her mind.

Angela   Last thing yer need when it's nearly yer time.

Eileen   I'm alright.

Angela   There's people being blown to pieces day and night and she can only think of herself. And she's the biggest ingrate with it. Know what she said to Vinnie when he mentioned moving in? She said she'd rather eat her own shite than live with him.

Eileen (*horrified*)   She never.

Angela   She did.

Eileen   She'll come round, in the end.

Angela   I very much doubt it.

Eileen   Any more tea in that pot?

Angela   We're out o' milk, mind.

Eileen   I don't mind it black.

Angela *exits.*

Eileen *is hit by a wave of sorrow.*

Angela *re-enters. She gives* **Eileen** *tea and a cigarette. They both light up.*

Angela   'Ere y'are, girl. Not too stewed.

Eileen   Lovely, ta.

Angela   She'll be alright when she's had a good cry.

Eileen   That's it.

Angela   Here you are, just widowed, and she can't show decent respect –

Eileen   She doesn't mean anything –

Angela   And here I am with one child hysterical and another one God knows where, lost to the world. Yer start to wonder what yer've done to deserve it, Eil.

Sounds off, the front door being opened. Men's voices, laughter.

About time an' all.

Eileen   Sounds like they've had a few.

Angela   They better not have.

Phelan *enters, accompanied by* **Colin**.

Phelan   Bloody 'ell, girl, yer'll never believe what we've just seen –

Colin   Never saw it comin' –

Angela   What?

Phelan   Yer think it's half a mile away –

Colin   It goes that quick –

Phelan   Next thing it's up yer arse and yer've gotta dive for dear life! Took the skin off me hands, look –

Angela *has a look at his bleeding palms.*

Angela   You'll live.

Phelan   Like Our Lord on the Cross here, aren't I?

Colin   Aye, yeah!

Angela   Ey. Don't start with the blasphemin'. What are yers on about, anyway?

Phelan   The ack-ack on wheels, that's what. Massive gun on the back of a lorry.

Angela   I'll put some calamine on for yer.

Phelan   Ah, leave it. Come 'ere –

He swings her round, she breaks free.

Angela   Ey! Don't you touch me. This was clean on today –

Phelan (*with a flash of charm*)   Just for me, ey? Aren't I the lucky one . . .

Angela   Get out and wash yer hands before they go septic.

Phelan   Clean hands is that what you like.

He goes.

Colin   There's more on the way tonight, Mrs D, no danger.

Angela   God help us.

Colin   Train full of ammunition gone up as well, down Edge Hill.

Angela   We're sittin' ducks here.

Colin   Got the bloody bit between the teeth, yer've gotta hand it to them –

Angela   Mind your language in my house, lad.

Colin   Yer what?

Angela   You heard.

Phelan *reappears, clocks the situation.*

Colin   I've only said 'bloody', aven't I –

Phelan   Ey. Button it.

Colin   Yer jokin', aren't yer –

Phelan   You'll apologise to Mrs Donohue.

Colin   Yer messin' –

Phelan   You'll apologise. Now.

Colin   Will I?

Phelan   Come 'ere –

Phelan *cuffs* **Colin** *on the side of the head, sending him reeling. The women scream.*

Colin   What's that for?

Phelan *kicks* **Colin***, he cries out.*

Phelan   That's for bein' a fuckin' smart alec. In future, you show Mrs Donohue proper respect and you don't answer back when she puts you right. Right?

Colin   Alright.

Phelan   Like I said. You'll apologise.

Colin   Sorry there, Mrs Donohue –

Angela   Right.

Theresa *re-enters.*

Phelan   Here she is. Alright there, queen?

Theresa   What's all the noise?

Angela   It's nothing, alright.

Theresa   Who's this?

Phelan   He's with me, isn't he?

Theresa   Oh aye. What d'yer call him then?

Phelan   Who?

Theresa   Yer monkey.

Phelan   Oh, him? Colin.

Theresa   Hello, Colin. Hope he's payin' yer well.

Phelan   Just had his weekly bonus.

Theresa   Oh aye.

Phelan   Dozen bananas.

He chuckles at his own joke.

Theresa   How much have you made out the navy this week then.

Phelan   Yer what?

Theresa   They been generous or what.

Colin   That's for us to know –

Phelan   I said button it, you –

Angela *reassures* **Phelan** *about* **Eileen**.

Angela   She's alright, Vin.

Theresa   Yeah. We're all friends here, Vinnie mate. She knows yer a robbin' bastard.

Phelan   Does she now. Fine. Good enough. Ey, listen, girl. Haven't seen yer, 'ave I, so . . . I'm awful sorry about Frank's grave and that. Shockin' that is.

Eileen   Why? What's happened to it?

Theresa *approaches* **Phelan**.

Angela   Wasn't gonna tell yer, Eil. Cemetery got bombed last night.

Eileen *gasps in horror. She feels this deeply.*

Angela   Arr don't, girl –

Theresa (*in* **Phelan**'s *face*)   D'yer know what? If I hear my father's name out of your mouth once more I'll fuckin' kill yer.

Phelan (*calmly*)   Yeah? You and whose army?

Theresa   You stink, d'yer know that? Like a dead body, you smell.

Phelan *laughs to himself as* **Theresa** *turns away.*

Phelan   Terrible, isn't it? Drop a bomb on the dear departed? Not nice. Not civil at all. One minute yer lyin' there snoozin' in yer shroud, yer pet worms quietly going about their business, then BAM! – you're scattered to the four winds –

Theresa   You've got it comin' to you, d'yer know that. In this life and the next.

Phelan   Ah, stop it now, queen, will yer? Yer puttin' the wind up me.

Theresa   Am I.

Phelan   The way she looks at me. Like I'm Satan himself with his flies undone.

Colin *laughs an odd sort of laugh.*

Phelan   What's ado with you?

Colin   Nothing.

Phelan   Better 'adn't be. Get the bag, will yer.

Colin *gets up.*

Angela   I can't face going to Anfield to see it. All them poor souls.

Phelan   Them poor gravediggers an' all.

Angela   Oh Jesus, don't tell me –

Phelan   Tell them what we heard in the Oak Tree, lad.

Colin   Oh aye, yeah. One of them was only just rescued out the Atlantic, been on a raft for nine days. His mate got him this job diggin' graves, just till he could get back on his feet –

Phelan   Talk about hard lines.

Exit **Colin**.

Phelan (*to* **Eileen**)   How's yer dad keepin', girl?

Eileen   He's not been too good, to be honest.

Phelan   Trouble with his pins, last I heard. Swollen up, aren't they.

Eileen   They are.

Phelan   Give him my best when yer see him, won't yer?

Angela   Vin – haven't had a chance to tell yer, have I – ?

Phelan   What?

Angela   Eileen's lost her Peter in the merchant navy –

Phelan   Oh no. Oh, I am sorry. (*To* **Angela**.) Why didn't yer say? What ship was he on, love?

Eileen   The *Anchises*.

Colin *reappears with an army-issue backpack, full and heavy.*

Phelan   How long were yers married?

Eileen   Fifteen months, nearly.

Phelan   Convoy, was it.

Eileen   Yeah.

Phelan   And you carryin an' all. I tell yer what, they're losing all their best men, their best ships. The way things are going, if they can't stop these bastard U-boats, there's nothin' down for arl England.

Angela   They're gonna starve us out.

Phelan   That's the way the wind's blowin'.

Theresa   If we're gonna stand a chance, firms like yours'll have to turn the repairs round good and quick, won't they?

Phelan   We do our bit, don't you worry about that.

Theresa   Oh aye, yeah.

Phelan (*to* **Eileen**)   Your fella was a brave man that's died for a great country, the greatest in the world, has been for donkey's. But this dog's had his day. A bigger dog's come to piss all over him.

Angela   Vinnie.

Phelan   What'll yer do now, girl. Stay with yer mam and dad, or what?

Eileen   Yeah.

Phelan   Ey, did I tell yer, they've let another load out the camp?

Angela   Which camp?

Colin   There's a camp in Huyton full of Germans and
Eyties.

Angela   Are you jokin' with me?

Eileen   I heard somethin' about that.

Phelan   Aliens they are – Jews and Communists.

Angela   And they've let them out?

Phelan   So keep yer eyes peeled.

Eileen *starts shifting to leave.*

Angela   That's all we need, isn't it.

Eileen   What do they look like?

Theresa   They've got two horns, like this, and a tail with a
fork on the end.

Phelan   We've all to report any suspicious activity.

Theresa   Is that right?

Angela (*to* **Eileen**)   Makin' a move, are yer, girl.

Eileen   Better had. Try and get me head down.

Phelan   Are yer alright for coupons, sweetheart?

Angela   She knows she only has to ask. I'll knock for yer if
there's a raid, alright?

Eileen   Alright then. T'ra.

General goodbyes.

Exit **Eileen**.

Angela   Poor little cow.

Colin   Everywhere yer go, someone's just heard someone's
copped it.

Angela   They were sayin' in the shelter, there's trains leavin'
town every night with piles of dead bodies.

Theresa   Trains to where?

Angela   Delamere Forest. They're puttin' them in mass graves.

Phelan   This is just the start of it.

Angela   Anyway, I thought the Jews were on *our* side.

Phelan   Well, that's half the problem, isn't it.

Colin   People thinkin' like that.

Angela   There's none round here, anyway.

Phelan   Course not, they've got the big houses down Woolton and Gateacre, 'aven't they.

Colin   It was the same over there till Hitler took over.

Angela   What's he gonna do with them?

Phelan   He'll get shot of them, won't he, sharpish.

Angela   How?

Phelan   He's decided they're inferior to us, and as such –

Angela   They can't be that inferior, can they.

Phelan   Ey?

Angela   If they're running everything.

Theresa   Jesus was a Jew.

Angela   How d'yer work that one out?

Theresa   On the Cross, wasn't it. King of the Jews.

Phelan   Aye, yeah, that's what the Romans called him, like –

Theresa   He was born a Jew. His mother was Jewish.

Angela   Go 'way. Our Lady?

Phelan   Listen, yer can't compare your modern-day Semite – When that refugee ship went down, the *Arandora Star* –

Colin   Refu-jew ship, more like.

Phelan   – they were chucking women and children out the lifeboats –

Angela   Ah, get lost –

Phelan   They were, girl. It's what they're like –

Colin   Hitler'll sort them out.

Angela   Well, I still don't agree with it.

Phelan   Well, yer can tell Adolf when yer see him, can't yer –

Air-raid warning sounds.

Angela   I will.

Phelan   That'll be him now!

Angela   Mother o' God. 'Ere we go again.

They all begin getting up to go to the shelter.

Colin   Told yers, didn't I.

Theresa   Don't forget Eileen.

Angela   What's the bettin' she's in the privy? Sure you're not comin'?

Theresa   I'll be alright.

Phelan   You won't be if yer catch one, girl.

Theresa   If I do, I do.

Angela   She's got a death wish.

Theresa   Smell in those places makes me sick. Either that or the bloody singing.

Angela   Killjoy.

Phelan   See yer, girl. Don't wait up!

Exit **Phelan**, *laughing and joking,* **Angela** *and* **Colin**.

Theresa   The fact he's even breathin' is my disgrace. And our Michael's. Every day he walks the earth is another black mark. I feel ashamed – ashamed I can't do it meself.

After the funeral he came back, friend of the family, pay
his respects. He kissed my cheek. Consolin' arm round me
mam. How long did they leave it before they started up again?
Sneak out the entry for a quickie durin' the wake?

It's not just what he's done that makes me want to kill him. It's
every bleedin' thing about him. *That makes me want to kill him.*
Listen to me. And me a May Queen an' all.

Come on, Hitler! Think you're cock o' the walk, do yer? Come
on then! Show us what yer made of! Rain down them bombs
and smash the lot of us!

Give us this day our daily hell.

A barrage of explosions ends the scene.

Scene Four

Huyton Woods.

Early afternoon sunshine through the trees.

Liliane *enters. She's very hungry and tired. She has a bruise on her face.
Her clothes are torn and there are bloodstains. She carries a pathetic
bundle – some underclothes, hairbrush, and so on. She was attacked last
night, and is still in pain. She walks slowly, gingerly.*

She sits, takes a hand-mirror from the bundle and examines the bruise.

*She starts to sing to herself – the Yiddish lullaby 'Raisins and Almonds'.
After just a few lines she is too upset to carry on.*

Liliane   The path is hard. The way is thick with thorns and
stinging plants. But I must walk it –

She goes.

Michael *and* **JJ** *enter.* **JJ** *carries a packet of bread and a billycan.*

JJ   What d'yer reckon – lush bit of grass here. Tree for a roof –

Michael   Here?

JJ   Yes, Michael. Here.

Michael   Nettles everywhere.

JJ   Christ's sake.

Michael   Try further on.

JJ drinks from the billycan.

JJ   Should've filled up at the brook –

Michael   Give it here.

JJ passes him the water – there's not much left.

JJ   Thought we were done with this lark, dodgin' and weavin', sleepin' rough.

Michael   Yeah, well.

JJ   Pair o' bloody tramps, that's what we are. That one night we had in the barracks was like I'd died and gone to heaven. A proper mattress! A pillow!

*He takes the bread from the packet – it's a small round loaf and he tears it in two, giving half to **Michael**. There's a pause while they eat . . .*

*JJ notices with a start the sorry figure of **Liliane** entering, head down.*

JJ   Oh Jesus.

She's like a startled deer when she notices them. Not sure whether to trust or run for her life.

*JJ goes to **Liliane**. She takes a step back.*

JJ   Are you alright – ?

Michael   Course she's not, state of 'er –

JJ   Somebody done this?

She nods a 'yes'.

'Ere y'are, sit down for a minute –

Liliane *flinches from him.*

Michael   We don't need this –

JJ   Easy – it's OK.

Michael   Got business, 'aven't we.

JJ   Take no notice to him. What's yer name?

No response. Short pause.

Michael   She's been raped, 'asn't she – ?

JJ   Michael – ! (*To* **Liliane**.) Y're alright. Why don't you sit down there for a minute, ey.

Michael   She's been fuckin' raped –

JJ   It's dry, honest – come on now.

He coaxes **Liliane** *to sit down.*

She watches them.

JJ   We won't hurt yer, promise.

Liliane *moves into a semi-supine position, still watchful.*

JJ   Go on.

She lies down, as if sinking into a warm bath. Closes her eyes.

Music – 'Raisins and Almonds' – soothes her.

Pause.

Michael   Think she's bleedin'? 'Ave a look.

JJ   Can't, can I – ?

Michael   This is all we need.

JJ   Can't just leave her, can we.

Michael   She's well out of it.

JJ   Shock, maybe.

Michael   Ask her where they went. Which way.

JJ   Can you say – Which way'd they go?

Michael   They might still be around, don't yer reckon – ?

JJ   I don't know, do I?

Michael   Fuckin' *bastards* –

He goes off to search.

JJ   Michael! What yer playin' at? Michael – ! (*To* **Liliane**.)
Here, got some water –

He gives her the billycan.

Listen, I've gotta look – See if you're still bleeding, alright?
I'm gonna look now. Alright?

He doesn't look.

If you can hear me. Open your eyes.

Liliane (*has a soft German – Munich – accent*)   Will you be kind?

JJ   I will be, definitely. I just wanna help yer, that's all.

Liliane   Really?

JJ   Cross me heart.

Liliane   Hungry.

JJ *gives her bread. She eats* . . .

Liliane   Your friend –

JJ   Don't worry about him.

Liliane   I'm not bleeding.

JJ   Are you sure, now. We'll get you a doctor –

Liliane   No doctor.

JJ   Alright. We're not gonna turn yer in, if that's what you're
worried about.

Liliane   Where is he?

JJ   He's lookin' for them.

Liliane   He's wasting his time.

JJ   You think so.

Liliane   It was hours ago.

JJ   Listen, did they –

Liliane   No. It wasn't going to happen to me. I fought him.
He was drunk.

Short pause. **JJ** *scans the woods.*

Liliane   Is he always like this?

JJ   Like what.

Liliane   He is very quick to be angry.

JJ   We were in France, in the fighting. We saw a lot of it then.

Liliane   A lot of what?

JJ   It's one of the first things, isn't it. They go for the women.
Use them up, throw them away.

Liliane   You saw this?

JJ   We never made it to Dunkirk. Took us a few months to
get back. So yeah, we saw a lot of things. Listen – are you –
German – or what? Can't be German. Dutch?

Liliane   German. German Jew. My name is Liliane.

Michael *enters, holding the gun.*

JJ   Jesus, Michael, what're yer playin' at, mate?

Michael   Thought I could catch up with them – alright?

JJ   No, mate, it's not alright, as it happens –

He takes **Michael** *to one side.*

JJ   I don't want to tell yer again. *That* is still with us for one
thing and one thing only.

Michael   Who is she then?

JJ   Just keep yerself together, will yer. Jesus.

Michael   Who is she?

JJ   Liliane. German Jew.

Michael   Oh aye. Enemy alien.

JJ   Explains the hidin', anyway. Says she wasn't, er – y'know.
That.

Michael *speaks to* **Liliane**.

Michael   German, are yer.

Liliane   From Munich, yes.

Michael   What yer doin' here, then.

Liliane   I came to England to find work. My brother and I.

Michael   Yer brother?

JJ   What's happened to him then.

Michael   D'you know where he is, like?

Liliane   He was in prison, at the Huyton camp, a couple of
miles from here. Then they put him on a ship to Canada. It
was sunk.

Pause.

JJ   So you were working.

Michael   What kind of work?

Liliane   I was in service, a doctor and his wife in Wavertree.
They were decent to me, let me play piano at their parties. But
when war came – they turned me in. They took my clothes,
books, everything. Since then – (*she shrugs*) – this is how I live.

Michael   This brother o' yours – what was he doin' here?

JJ   Leave her, will yer.

Michael   I'm only askin'.

JJ   She's lost him, hasn't she. Just been near killed herself. (*To*
Liliane.) Where are yer on yer way to now?

She shrugs.

What'll yer do with yerself.

Liliane   Try and stay alive. This is what we all must do.

Michael   Good luck to yer then. (*To* **JJ**.) Come 'ead.

JJ   Hold yer horses, will yer. (*To* **Liliane**). Can you stand up?

She stands, with difficulty. **JJ** *steadies her at the elbow.*

Michael   What are yer playin' at, J.

JJ   I'm not leavin' her here like this.

Michael   Are you jokin' with me?

JJ   All I'm sayin' is, let her bivvy up with us while she gets her breath back. Imagine if this was your Theresa, ey?

Michael   It's not.

JJ   Them people who helped us – Bernard, Justine – this is nothin' compared to them, is it.

No response.

Think about that gun then, ey –

Michael *flares – not with anger, but the memory of something very dark. He might draw his fist as if to hit* **JJ** *for reminding him.*

JJ   Alright! Sorry. But – just look at her, will yer.

Michael   Alright – Alright. Jesus' sake.

They gather themselves to move off. **JJ** *supports* **Liliane**.

JJ   Easy does it.

Michael   Come 'ead then, if yer coming.

JJ   This way.

Scene Five

After the all-clear has sounded.

Theresa *is collecting things into a basket to take to the cemetery for a makeshift memorial – a pair of shoes, a shaving brush and so on.*

She takes a pair of scissors, cuts a little length of hair from her head, places it in the basket.

At this point **Phelan** *enters.*

Phelan   Alright, girl.

Theresa *ignores him.*

Phelan   Yer been alright?

Murder out there, tellin' yer. Gorgeous spring day and there's bloody mayhem all over the shop. Every other street, something's been flattened. That church n' all – what's-its-name –

Theresa *tenses, hoping it's not her own . . .*

Phelan   Top of Bold Street. Gone up like a bommie, apparently.

Theresa *is looking through a box or drawer.*

Phelan   Yer mam's gone to queue up at Freddie's. Said to tell yer she'll be back about five.

Well, I'm beat. Gonna get a quick shave, then get me head down for half an hour.

He starts undressing.

Theresa? A 'hello' would be nice. D'yer know what – one of these days yer'll crack a smile and the heavenly choirs'll start up with the hallelujahs. The cherubim and seraphim'll be dancin' in the aisles. Well, a fella can dream, can't he?

What've yer lost, anyway?

Theresa   Is there a picture of me in a veil in me mam's room.

Phelan   In a veil?

Theresa   Yes, in a veil. Jesus, are yer deaf?

Phelan   Oh aye, yeah – so there is. On the dressin' table.

Theresa *gets up, goes to the bedroom.*

Phelan   Least I think it is . . .

Shirt undone, he comes to have a casual look at the contents of the basket.

He raises his voice to be heard off.

This yer da's paraphernalia, is it? Not givin' these the Sally Army, are yer? Yer mam won't be too pleased –

Theresa *re-enters with the picture.*

Theresa   I'm taking them to the cemetery.

Phelan   Oh aye. What for?

Theresa   What for? Don't believe this. Because – because your mates up there have blasted me dad's coffin –

Phelan   They're no mates o' mine –

Theresa   They killed him the first time *apparently* but they've come back to make sure. ENEMY ACTION, remember?

Phelan   Course I do. Fuckin' tragedy.

Theresa   Walkin' down the Dock Road mindin' his own business and a bomb landed on him, isn't that the story? That's the story, am I right?

Phelan   Like I said –

Theresa   Yeah, like you said. So we put him in the ground. 'Night, God bless. Now there's no'n there to say he's even ever existed. But at least if people see these, they might go, ''Ere y'are, look, Frank was here. Look, there's a picture of his daughter – his son's call-up letter – oh and that'll be his shaving brush, his pipe, one of his belts – '

Phelan (*holding the picture*)   You're not takin' this, are yer. Yer mam'll go sparc.

Theresa   She'll be glad to see the back of it.

Phelan   How d'yer work that one out?

Theresa   I'm Daddy's girl, know what I mean?

She squares up to him.

Daddy's girl.

Pause.

Phelan   We're gonna have to have words, you and me.

Theresa   Words. Yeah. Let's have some words, why not.

Phelan   Yer know – your mother could do with yer bein' a bit more – civil.

Theresa   Oh, d'yer reckon?

Phelan   I do, yeah. Yer arl fella's gone, it's a terrible bleedin' shame – serious now, not coddin' yer, I had a lot of time for Frank. Listen – we grew up together, him and me – you know as well as I do I put a fair bit of work his way over the years, things could've been hard for yers all –

Theresa   Give me strength –

Phelan   I'm just sayin', there's a history there, isn't there? We had our differences, sure –

Theresa   Differences.

Phelan   Who doesn't. But now he's gone, well – there's nothin' none of us can do about it, is there. I know you loved the bones of yer dad, but the way you take it out on yer mam –

Theresa   The way I take *what* out on her?

Pause.

Phelan   All I'm sayin' is – you don't like me. Fair enough. I'm the wicked stepfather or whatever –

Theresa   Don't use that word.

Phelan   Just – she's still grievin' as well, yer know.

Theresa   Is she now?

Phelan   Yes, she is. And she could do without her daughter –

Theresa   That why you're here, is it? To help her get over me dad? That what it's all about, the coupons and the fivers and – every'n else you give her!

Phelan   You're out of order, girl.

Theresa   You're the one who wanted words. Here's a few more for yer, Vinnie — I hope you burn in hell.

Phelan   You're yer own worst enemy, d'yer know that — ?

Theresa (*prepares to leave*)   That's where yer wrong, Vinnie, mate. *You're* my worst enemy. And yer always will be, d'you hear? Till my last breath. Or yours. Whichever comes first.

She exits. **Phelan** *pauses, then goes.*

Scene Six

Anfield Cemetery.

Michael *enters.* **Liliane** *follows behind.*

Where he expected to see his father's grave, there is a crater.

When she sees the pit, **Liliane** *utters in German expressions of shock and horror.*

We see **Michael** *grapple with the enormity of what's happened. He prowls around the edge of the crater.*

Michael   YOUR LOT DID THIS! FUCKING GERMANS DID THIS!

But he's not really angry with her. From the fact that she reacts only with kindness and concern we can tell a bond has developed. He is in some kind of torment.

She catches up with him, but when she tries to comfort him he resists.

Get *off*, will yer. Don't touch me. Said don't *touch* me —

But it doesn't last long. He lets her hold him, shush him . . .

Gone — Nothing left — Jesus! I thought — if I could at least see where they put him —

Liliane   I'm so sorry. It's so terrible for you.

Michael   You've got no fuckin' idea.

Liliane   No. To lose your father in this way. I can't imagine.
You must go home, see your mother, your sister –

Michael *bridles at the word 'home', breaks away from her.*

Liliane   What was his name? Your father's name.

Michael   Frank.

Liliane *picks up a stone, places it on the edge of the pit.*

Liliane   Frank. His memory be blessed.

She sets about gathering stones and placing them on the edge.

Michael   What are yer doing?

Liliane   To make a mark. To show we remember. There
must have been hundreds of people here –

Michael   Dead bodies, is all.

Liliane   Don't say that. They were people. If they are gone,
still we remember.

Pause.

So many!

Michael   Don't worry about it, Lili – soon be full again,
won't it. Plenty more where they came from.

Liliane   I'm thinking – how many died from the bombs. Like
your father.

Michael   He was murdered.

Liliane   What did you say?

Michael   I said, he was murdered. By me mother's – Me
mother was shaggin' a mate of me dad's, wasn't she. He walked
in on them. Bang.

Pause. **Liliane** *goes towards him.*

Michael   I've come back to sort him out.

Liliane   Sort him out?

Michael   You wanna know all the details, do yer?

Liliane   No. You don't have to tell me. Of course.

Michael   What.

Liliane   I think – I think I understand now.

Michael   Do yer.

Liliane   I think so, yes.

Michael   So what the fuck's goin' on then? Tell me, cos I'd love to know.

Liliane   This is – This is a disaster for you.

Michael   That's about the size of it, mate.

Liliane   I don't know what I can say.

Michael   Nothin' much yer can say, is there. Nothin' much to be said.

Liliane   You want to have revenge.

Michael   Too right I do.

Liliane   JJ – did he really go to his cousin?

Michael   None of your business –

Liliane   Has he gone to do it? Has he?

Michael   Hope not. That's my job.

Michael *hears the drunken singing of* **Mickey**, *a gravedigger, approaching.*

Liliane   Your *job*?

Michael   Someone comin'.

Exit **Lili** *and* **Michael**.

Mickey *enters, singing.*

He's trailing a spade in one hand and carrying a bottle in the other. He brandishes the spade like a bayonet.

Mickey   Who goes there? Friend or Fritz! And if yer've got some, show us yer tits –

In the shame of the father, and of the son, and all the bloody ghosts –

See them in the explosions, don't yer, in the flames n'all –

On guard, yer blaggards! Don't scare me, none o' yers! Come 'ead! I'll rearrange yer features for yer, alright! Come 'ead!

He lunges with the spade at an imaginary foe, and falls over. Lying down, he is somewhat calmer. Laughs to himself, points to the sun.

Ey! Put that light out! Tryna get me 'ead down 'ere, aren' I! Put that bloody light out!

He loves this joke, laughs helplessly.

Sometimes – it's true – I drink to forget. But I never forget to drink. *L'chaim! Slainte! Prost!*

He drinks.

Oh – that's hit the sweet spot.

> 'Wine can of their wits the wise beguile
> Make the sage frolic, and the serious smile.'

The Pope said that, so he did, and who are we to disagree? Who are *we*? He's inflammable. Can't put a foot wrong if he tries. We're just ants, aren't we, crawlin' round his size nines.

That's how we found Kevin and Stephen, when we was sortin' out the mess. The only ones with their bloody boots on, weren't they.

Posh voice.

Bottoms up!

He takes a big swig. Then starts singing again. Then breaks off.

They've hit the big library in William Brown Street, y'know. Oh aye. All them books I meant to read. *Wuthering Heights*, Charles Dickens, all gone. How'm I gonna get meself edjumacated now, ey? Big reader, me. Just finished a cowie – get them off a fella in Church Street – *The Ox-Bow Incident*. Yer

read it? It's cracker. They're tryna find out who murdered –
erm – thingy, so they get up a posse, y'know. They lynch these
three fellas, turns out they didn' even do it.

During the following **Theresa** *enters, finds a spot, starts unpacking her
box of* **Frank**'s *belongings.*

Mickey   Was murder at the 'ozzie last night n' all, our
Maureen said. They was operatin' on some poor Greek
bastard, a seaman. His stomach's hangin' out and they're tryna
save him, like. He's out cold under the gas, like a side o' ribs on
the butcher's slab, know wharra mean? Showin' everything he's
got. Anyway, this screamer comes in and flattens the wing. The
surgeon there, Irish fella, knife at the ready – *he's* gone. The
sister, standin' there with the tray of instruments – she's gone.
But the Greek? He's slept through the whole thing, hasn't he?
They throw him in the back of a meat wagon, take him to
Fazak. They stitch him up, he wakes up none the wiser –

He sees **Theresa**.

Mickey   Aye aye, who's the dame?

Theresa   Alright, mate.

Mickey   Alright yerself.

Theresa   D'you work here?

Mickey   Me? Do I look like a gravedigger?

Theresa   I'd say so, yeah.

Mickey   For all you know I might be a German who's been
shot down in flames.

Theresa   Yer don't sound very German.

Mickey   Ditched in the Mersey, didn' I, swallowed the water.

Theresa   That right? So *eine kleine Musik ist verboten*, don't you
reckon?

Beat. **Mickey** *concedes.*

Mickey   Alright, you win. I'm – erm, Norwegian.

Theresa   Get lost.

Mickey   We invented Scouse.

Theresa   One o' Quisling's lot then, are yer.

Mickey   Ey? Who's he when he's at home.

Theresa   Fascist.

Mickey   Oh.

Theresa   Traitor. .

Mickey   Oh.

Theresa   Sold his people to the SS.

Mickey   No! None of that. No truck with that. I'm out of a peace-loving tribe of Norwegian scavengers, aren't I, like a kind o' conchie Viking, y'know, roamin' the high seas in search of, erm . . . something. Things we like. See, yer've confused me now with them bad words. I'm not a fascist, alright?

Su'm's crawled up your drawers, I can tell.

Theresa   'As it. So what's with the spade then, Quisling.

Mickey   Arr, don't call me that, will yer, girl. Anything else. Grizzling. Sizzling.

Theresa   Ugly duckling.

Mickey   That'll do.

Theresa   Yer diggin' for victory, are yer?

Mickey   Buried treasure.

Theresa   Is that right?

Mickey   Always fancied bein' a pirate, me.

Theresa   A Norwegian pirate.

Mickey   *Robinson Crusoe*'s me favourite book.

Theresa   Figures.

Mickey   How's that?

Theresa   Yer look like a Billy-no-mates.

Mickey   No man is an island. Except our Billy, obviously.

Theresa   And Jack Jones.

Mickey   And poor Robinson, God love him.

Theresa   Just a parrot for company.

Mickey   Don't forget Friday.

Theresa   Half past eight outside the Grafton.

Mickey   I'll wear that dress you like.

Pause.

What's in the box?

Theresa   Got some treasure of me own, haven't I?

Mickey   I get yer.

Theresa   Me dad was here. Francis Donohue.

Mickey   That's hard cheese.

He gives her the bottle, she drinks.

When did he clock in, queen?

Theresa   November. He was next to me nan and grandad.

Mickey (*remembers*)   Donohues. Yeah . . . Sorry about all this. Bit of a mess, like.

Theresa   Not your fault is it.

Mickey   This time next week it'll be like it never 'appened, promise yer.

Theresa   Will yer put these in the ground for us?

Mickey   Some of his things.

Theresa   Pathetic, isn't it.

Mickey   No, sweetheart. If it's good enough for the pharaohs –

Theresa *gestures, 'What?'*

Mickey   The pyramids was full of all their arl junk, wasn't it? 'Ad it bricked in with them, didn't thee, in case there was extra time and penalties.

Theresa   Take your word for it.

Mickey (*taking the box*)   Got a plan back in the yard. X marks the spot, ey, girl.

Theresa   Yeah.

Mickey   There's a charge, like.

Theresa   What kind of charge?

Mickey   A kiss.

Theresa   Yer cheeky get –

Mickey   The cheek's fine, I don't mind.

Theresa *comes and kisses him on the cheek. Then she goes.*

Mickey *picks up his spade, heads off. He looks up at the sun . . .*

Mickey   Ey! I won't ask you again! Bleedin' nuisance. Wanna get us *all* killed, do yer? I'm goin' the yard for a kip, and by the time I wake up you'd better 'ave that light out. Or I'll *report yer*. Alright? I'll report yer.

Exit.

Scene Seven

The Donohues' front room.

JJ *wears a black armband.*

Eileen *comforts* **Angela**. **Phelan** *looks on.*

JJ   There were the five of us. Me and your Michael, Johnny Bingham who we knew from our unit, but not all that well, fella called Simon, tank driver whose ankle was broke, and the Captain.

We'd found Simon next to his Matilda, been taken out by a
Panzer, but he'd been thrown clear. Rest of the crew . . . well,
there was not'n down for them. Simon's ankle was bust like I
say, and his hair was burned on one side. He couldn't believe
he was still alive . . . and if you'd seen the state of that Matilda
nor would you.

The Captain was alright, liked him meself but Michael didn't
warm to him much. He was called Avery or Avebury or
something like that. Michael didn't trust any of the officer class
as far as he could throw them, to be honest. Which was fair
enough considerin' the number o' daft orders we'd been given
by the likes. Well, we were in a bad way, we were all of us out
on our feet. And we could hear them, couldn't we, the German
tanks, steamin' through the country all around – put the fear o'
God in us.

The Captain hadn't got a clue, but yer couldn't blame him.
Michael was sure we could shimmy our way back north and
find our unit, or at least some other stragglers like us who might
at least have a radio. But cos o' Simon we couldn't go none too
quick, so we found a ditch and grabbed some kip till nightfall.

Horrible few hours that was, lyin' there listenin' to the panzers
on the grind. Soon as it was dark enough we packed up and
moved off, takin' turns – about carryin' Simon. Bastard moon
came up so we still had to keep tight to the hedges.

Anyway we'd been goin' about two hours when we saw this
sign – 'Paradise'. 'Le Paradise'. Captain called it 'para-dee'.
Tiny place, maybe ten houses, the church, cemetery, that was
about it. Me and the Captain went forward on a recce and
left the others in the churchyard. Last thing I said to your
Michael –

Angela *cries out,* **Phelan** *gestures to* **JJ** *to carry on.*

JJ   Said to him before I went, 'Keep your head down, soft
lad.' And he said, 'I will do.' That was the last time I saw him
alive.

Angela   O Jesus God have mercy.

Eileen   Oh, Angela.

Phelan   Go on, lad. She's alright.

Short pause.

JJ   The Captain and me, we found some food in this house, no one around. Then we saw these – these graves just been dug. One massive grave in fact it was, maybe fifty feet long –

Angela's *grief has burst its banks, and she cries out.* **JJ** *breaks off.*

Phelan   Hey

Angela   Mother o' God help me

Phelan   Angela – queen

Angela   I'm a dead woman

Phelan   No, love

Angela   D'yers hear me

Phelan   No

Eileen   Angela, don't

Angela   Dead to yers all

Eileen   Don't say that

Phelan   No one's that

Angela   How can I live now, ey

Tell me that

How can I

Phelan   No, love, come here

Angela   I gave birth

Phelan   Come here, let me now

Angela   I gave birth to him

Phelan   Come on, let me

Angela   Gone he's

Dead oh

Mother o' God.

Eileen   Don't, Angela

Angela   Why am I even

JJ   Mrs Donohue –

Angela   Why am I still breathin'

JJ   Michael was –

Angela   When he's dead

JJ   Mrs Donohue –

Angela   When he's

Eileen   Angela, he wants to

Angela   My son

Eileen   Angela

Angela   My only

Eileen   What did you want to say?

Angela   My only son oh God

Eileen   Did you want to say, JJ

Angela   Michael

I never meant

Phelan   God help her

Eileen   Here now

Angela   I want him

I want him Eileen

I want him back

Phelan   Come here

Angela   Michael

JJ   I'm so sorry, I really am –

Angela   My baby, my baby

JJ   There was nothing anyone could –

Angela   Baby boy

Phelan   Come on now

Angela   Get off you

Phelan   Hey

Angela   Get off

Phelan   Come on queen

Eileen   Angela

Angela   Don't you fuckin' queen me

Phelan   Hey

Angela (*to* **JJ**)   And how dare *you* –

Angela *attacks* **JJ**.

Eileen   No

Angela   God FORGIVE YOU

Phelan   HEY, I said

Angela   Yer fuckin' no-mark

Eileen   No

Leave him

Phelan   No bleedin' need, is there

Theresa *enters unnoticed*.

Angela   What gives you the right, ey?

Eileen   *Leave* him, he's done nothing.

Phelan   Alright, lad.

Angela   Come in 'ere, tell me my baby's –

Phelan   Yer alright, son

Eileen   Sit down, Ange

Angela   *You* saved *your*self

Phelan   Enough

Eileen   Sit down will yer now

Angela   God forgive yer

Cos *I won't*

Phelan   Quiet

Angela   Like yer father before yer

A waste o' space

Eileen   Stop it now

Angela   A fuckin' useless waste o' space

Phelan   No need I said

JJ   I'm sorry. I had to.

Phelan   She knows.

Eileen   Yer alright John.

Phelan   Give the lad a drink.

Eileen *sees* **Theresa** *come striding forward.*

Eileen   Oh my God!

Theresa *takes her mother by the shoulders, shakes her violently.*

A beat.

Then she slaps her, viciously.

Three or four beats.

Then **Theresa** *falls, sobbing, onto her mother's breast, and they cry together.*

Interval.

Scene Eight

Huyton Woods, as the planes drone above.

Michael *and* **Liliane** *sitting on the ground.*

Michael The worst part was Paris. People were panickin' – was in their faces, the way they talked, even if you hadn't got a clue what they were sayin', know wharra mean?

Liliane I do, yes –

Michael Your lot were bein' given new ID to say they were Jews. Places were being raided left, right and centre. We thought we were bound to get caught, just a matter of time.

Liliane The Maquis saved you.

Michael Even then – It was hard. They took us far as they could, we still had to walk for three weeks to get to the border, through freezing rain most of the time. By the time we got across, the pair of us had trench foot – swollen up, like.

Liliane Do you know what happened to Simon?

Michael The Maquis were takin' him to one of their hidey-holes, said they could maybe get him to a hospital down south, he spoke enough of the lingo for them to pass him off as one of theirs.

Liliane You have to tell someone about Paradis.

Michael *(scoffs)* Tell who?

Liliane It was – how to say – a war crime.

Michael The fact they shoot prisoners is why we're at war with them, isn't it. They're animals. The men in the field know that.

Liliane People should know –

Michael Look. No one's interested in what I've seen.

Liliane I think you're wrong.

Michael Please yerself. Pass the water, will yer.

Pause.

What was your brother's name?

Liliane Felix. But he was not so lucky.

Michael *doesn't get it.*

Liliane It means 'lucky one'.

Michael Right. No. Not a nice way to go, that. Sorry for yer.

Liliane I have a picture –

She digs into her bundle to retrieve a dog-eared photo.

Michael Older or younger?

Liliane Neither. I came five minutes before him, so I suppose –

Michael *raises a hand to stop her: he hears something. A woman singing. He girds himself for fight or flight, but* **Liliane** *is calm – she knows who it is.*

Liliane No – be still. I know this woman. Don't frighten her.

Veronica *enters. She wears a headscarf, carries a set of rosary beads, and singing a hymn to the Virgin Mary.*

Liliane Is it you, Veronica? It's very nice to cross your path again. How are you?

Veronica Oh, Lili.

Liliane The kids, is it.

Veronica Just for a change, ey? D'you see them yet? Been bleedin' everywhere, 'aven' I – seen hide nor hair.

Liliane I'm sorry.

Veronica Tellin' yer, when I get a hold of the swines their lives won't be worth livin'.

Liliane Remind us, where did you see them last?

Veronica   They was playin' in the back entry, weren't thee,
our Mags comes in for a drink o' water, sayin' they were off
to see the barrage balloons go up, and would I come. As if I
'adn't got better things to do. Who's yer fella?

Liliane   This is Michael.

Veronica   Alright, Michael.

Michael   Alright.

Veronica   You 'aven't seen two kids on yer travels, 'ave yer,
lad? Joseph's seven, about so high, curly mop, not a pick on
'im. Margaret's nine and a half, straight black hair tied back,
navy blue pinny – Well, if yer do see them, smack their arses
and tell them to get home quick for more of the same.

Michael   OK, I will do, yeah.

Veronica   Well, this isn't gettin' me messages in, is it? Nice
seein' yer again, Lili. You take care now. You gonna make an
honest woman of her then, Michael?

Michael   Don't know about that.

Veronica   Lovely girl like Lili all on her ownsome, not right,
is it. Am I embarrassin' yers now. Come round to ours after, Lil,
we'll 'ave a ciggie and a gab. You can teach them urchins
o' mine some of yer lovely manners. Nice to meet you, Michael.
Are yer a good lad, are yer?

Michael   Me?

Veronica   Yes, you.

Michael   Not really, no –

Veronica   I beg to disagree. See it in yer eyes. There's some
lowlifes out there, but you're not one of them. You'll do. T'ra
now.

Liliane   Veronica – wait.

Wordlessly, **Liliane** *asks* **Michael** *if she can give* **Veronica** *some
bread and water.* **Michael** *assents,* **Liliane** *offers them to* **Veronica**,
who pockets the bread, drinks from the billycan.

Veronica   I'm gonna say one for yers. One for the road, protect us –

She kneels.

Hail, holy Queen Mother of Mercy
Our life, our sweetness and our hope
To thee do we cry
Poor banished children of Eve
To thee do we send up our sighs.

Turn then, most gracious advocate
Thine eyes of mercy toward us.
O clement, O loving O sweet Virgin Mary
Pray for us, holy Mother of God –

And she prompts **Liliane** –

Liliane
That we may be worthy of the promises of Christ.

Veronica
Sweet Queen of Heaven,
Empress of the Marshes of Hell,
Look after my daughter Maggie and my son Joseph
Keep them safe from harm,
Safe in your loving arms for ever and ever –

Liliane   Amen.

Michael   Amen.

Veronica *rises.*

Veronica   Be good, now. If you can't be good, be careful. See yer, Lili, hon.

Liliane   See you – take care –

Veronica *goes.*

Michael   What was all that about?

Liliane   Her children –

Michael   What about them.

Liliane   They were killed three weeks ago.

Michael (*shocked and upset*)   Oh Christ –

Liliane   They were sleeping, a parachute bomb hit the street. She was at work, the early shift. Her husband is in the army.

Michael   So much fucking shit, everywhere – !

Liliane   What do you say – we are up to our eyes in it, no?

He lies down, closes his eyes. Pause.

Michael, I must ask –

Michael   Some peace and quiet, do you mind?

Liliane   Please. When you go to the house – *your* house –

Michael   What did I just say?

Liliane   Forgive me.

Long pause. **Michael** *tries in vain to rest,* **Lili**'s *questions hanging in the air.*

A distraction as she paces or brushes her hair, awaiting her moment to ask . . .

Liliane   Why did you really come back?

Michael   You know why.

Liliane   I'm not sure I do.

Michael   Gonna tell them what's what, aren't I.

Liliane   What is what.

Michael   They murdered me dad, didn't they? So they've got it comin'.

Liliane   Eye for eye, tooth for tooth.

Michael   Round 'ere we call it comeback. Yer dish it out, it comes back to yer.

Liliane   I see.

Michael   Do yer? Do yer really? Then why yer lookin' at me like I'm a piece of shite on yer shoe?

Liliane   You and JJ. You will not do this, I think.

Michael   You reckon.

Liliane   The idea of you –

Michael   He's a dead man, dug his own grave. I'm just helpin' him into it –

Liliane   To do it – it makes you the same.

Michael   Don't believe this. So – what – I should just turn the other cheek, should I?

Liliane   For fifteen minutes you will be glad. Then the shame will start to kill *you* –

Michael   The shame? What about the shame of him gettin' away with it –

Liliane   For the rest of your life you would be a murderer – like him.

Michael   Like *him*. Like *him* . . .

Where's *your* dad, Liliane. Ey? Is he safe, d'yer reckon? What if he isn't? What then?

Liliane   We all have our disasters. The task is to survive them, not to make some more.

Michael   I'll tell you a story, shall I? You'll like this. Last summer, middle of French fuckin' nowhere, right, thunderstorm, proper scary one – me and J are lookin' for shelter. We get to this barn, and just as we're about to go in we hear so'me – there's a girl in there fightin' for her life, tryin' to scream, and a man, a German, hittin' her and tellin' her to be quiet. We freeze. We don't know what to do. We're not armed, he probably is.

So we're standin' there listenin', like a pair o' kids outside the parents' bedroom – is Daddy hurtin' Mummy? Well, we knew he was, but there was not'n we could do about it –

Then there's a shot. And then it's quiet. Except for the sound of him fuckin' her.

Liliane *lets out a horrified gasp.*

Michael   He's killed her and he's carried right on. He's enjoyin' himself, isn't he.

We did nothing.

When he finally left, we went in, couldn't help ourselves, could we –

He is struggling to stay together. He takes the gun out of his pack.

This is his gun. He'd left it – he'd left it stuck inside her.

Michael *is overcome.*

Liliane *comes to him.*

Michael   So – have I got you right? You sayin' I'm the same as him as well? Are yer?

Liliane (*so sorry for him*)   Of course not – of course not –

Michael   Shoulda done so'me –

Liliane   He was an animal, as you say. The beast in the man. You could not do anything. Hush now.

Pause.

I will say something to you. OK?

Michael   OK.

Liliane   Your mother.

Michael   Me mother.

Liliane   When you do this thing.

Michael   She'll have to live with it, won't she.

Liliane To *live with it*? I'm not sure you know what you are saying.

JJ *enters.*

JJ   Alright?

Michael   Yeah – you?

JJ   Just about, yeah.

Michael   So what's the score?

JJ   Like we thought.

Michael   He's moved in.

JJ   Feet under the table. Razor by the sink.

Michael   Man and wife.

JJ   Looked like it to me.

Michael   Theresa?

JJ   Mate – she's goin' through it alright. You seen the grave, didn't yer. And then the news from me. Her head's wrecked.

Michael   She's not gone soft then.

JJ   No way.

Michael   And me mam?

JJ   She screamed the house down. She went for me n' all, called me for everything. Phelan tried to quiet her down but she was havin' none of it. Gotta tell yer, they didn't look such a happy couple by the time I left.

Michael   No. Well.

JJ   Havin' a wake for yer tomorrow night, believe it or not. At the Oak Tree.

Michael   Jesus.

JJ   We should do it after that. They'll all be half cut.

Michael   We'll talk about it. (*To* **Lili**.) Come on then,
Fräulein. Shake a leg. We're off.

Liliane   Where are we going?

Michael   Round the bend.

Liliane   The bend? Where?

JJ   He's messin' with yer. There's a soup kitchen not far off.
Need to keep our strength up, don't we?

They go.

Scene Nine

Angela *is lying on the floor,* **Phelan** *hovering near her. They've been
talking for a while, going round in circles. It might be good if we get the
idea they've drunk a fair bit – perhaps slurring or stumbling over words.*

Phelan   We're just goin' round in circles here. Just for a
fuckin' change. If you won't even let me near yer –

Angela   I don't want yer touchin' me.

Phelan   No. Why would yer.

Funny, isn' it – the idea was to make yer happy – you and me.
Can't even remember what the word *means* –

Angela   That's right. *You're* the one worse off –

Phelan   Ah, fuck this –

Angela   Yer never could stand him. You're glad he's dead,
admit it.

Phelan   Just bein' stupid now, aren't yer.

Angela   Yeah. Stupid. That's me. That's me alright –

Phelan   Arr for Christ's sake –

Angela   Me all over! –

A new wave of crying overtakes her.

Phelan   Come on. Yer must've known, deep down, like –

Angela   Must've known what?

Phelan   That he wasn't comin' back, God love him. I did like him, yer know I did. Awkward little bastard that he was. Knew him since he was in short pants, didn' I. Jealous of me from the kick-off.

Angela   He was.

Phelan   If I was kiddin' around with yer or with Theresa – he worshipped his sister, didn' he –

Angela   They was always thick as thieves.

Phelan   Now he's gone, it's a terrible fuckin' blow, I don't undermine it for a minute. Come on.

Pause.

Angela   I'm being punished.

Phelan   Arr no, don't go down that road, girl –

Angela   God's punishin' me –

Phelan   As if.

Angela   What we did –

Pause.

Phelan   I wish to Christ it hadn't happened, yer know I do – I just hit him that hard –

Angela *cries out.*

Phelan   – the way his head hit the grate –

Angela   Don't!

Pause.

We should've hanged for it.

Phelan   Ah, Jesus' sake –

Angela   Lyin' there bleedin' to death – I did nothing. The path was set from then.

Phelan   What path's that, the garden path?

Angela   I wish I'd never started with yer, Vinnie – miserable whore that I am –

Phelan   Ah, that's right – Michael's copped it cos you were playin' away from home –

Angela   Shut up, will yer –

Phelan   We get caught, what happens to yer kids *then*? 'There they go,' people'd say. 'D'yer know their mam was hanged in Walton?'

Angela *is sobbing to herself.*

Phelan   Yeah – that's it. Have a good wallow.

Angela   Fuck off.

Phelan   Yer what?

Angela   You heard.

Phelan   I give up.

Pause.

I'll stay at mine tonight then, will I.

Angela   Do what yer like. Yer always do.

Phelan   Obvious you need to be on yer own.

Angela   Is it.

Phelan (*getting ready to leave*)   Try and get some kip, will yer. There's the wake tomorrer. I'll be round about four. Alright?

No response. **Phelan** *leaves.*

Angela *drags herself up off the floor and wanders the room, listless and adrift. She might be praying, silently. She lies down again.*

A pause. Darkness thickens.

Out of the shadows, **Father Quiggan** *appears to* **Angela**.

Father Quiggan   How long has it been since your last confession?

Angela *cannot speak.*

Father Quiggan   Tell me your sins, child.

Angela   I'm ashamed –

Father Quiggan   It's only words now. Say the words.

A distant explosion.

Angela   Why do I have to?

Father Quiggan   Because you will burn otherwise. The pain of your first labour.

Michael *appears.*

Angela   Oh, Michael –

Father Quiggan   You were only a girl.

Angela   His head soaked in my blood –

Father Quiggan   He fought to get out.

Angela   I near died of him –

Father Quiggan   Times that pain by a thousand. And it goes on forever.

The whistle of a bomb falling. A huge explosion. The sound of breaking glass, debris falling.

Angela   Oh, Jesus wept –

Phelan *enters, goes straight to* **Angela**, *starts groping her.*

Father Quiggan   November.

Michael   What the fuck's this?

Phelan   What's it look like.

Michael *reaches to touch the top of his head – when he takes it away it's covered in blood.*

Father Quiggan   Poor Frank.

Angela   Blood comin' out of yer eye.

Father Quiggan   There is an avenging angel.

A burst of heavy machine-gun fire, and a teenage girl laughing.

Angela   Oh God –

Father Quiggan   Bow down.

Enter the **Virgin.**

The **Virgin** *approaches* **Angela.**

Angela *is terrified.*

Father Quiggan *has a jar of ashes, and the* **Virgin** *touches the ashes with the forefinger and middle finger of her right hand.*

Father Quiggan   The ashes of him you killed.

The **Virgin** *raises her fingers in blessing.*

Father Quiggan   You once were dust. You will be dust again.

The **Virgin** *marks* **Angela***'s forehead.*

Father Quiggan   Your son will see the fires of Hell. And he's bringing it all back home.

The **Virgin** *walks slowly away from* **Angela***, exits.*

Deafening sound of a dive-bomber coming in to attack, machine-gun fire.

Angela   How can he be?!

Father Quiggan   Here it comes – Get down!

No one moves.

Angela   How can he be, if he's dead!

JJ *enters.*

Phelan *punches* **Michael***, kicks him when he's down.*

Father Quiggan *turns his back, and walks away.*

Phelan *starts dragging* **Michael** *off by the feet.*

JJ   I'm sorry, Mrs D. There's nothin' down for yer.

Angela   What d'yer mean? Where are yer takin' him?

Phelan (*as he drags* **Michael** *off*)   There's bombs fallin' all over. No one'll know any different –

Theresa *enters.*

Angela   Can't give him a proper burial –

Theresa   Yer gave me dad one of those, and look what happened to *him* –

JJ   Said to him before I went, 'Keep your head down, soft lad.' And he said, 'I will do.'

He sings. **Theresa** *joins in.*

> The first I met was a grey-haired father
> Searching for his only son
> I said 'Old man, there's no use searching
> For up to Heaven your son has gone.'

> The old man cried out broken-hearted
> Bending o'er I heard him say
> 'I knew my son was too kind-hearted
> I knew my son would never yield.'

> The last I met was a dying rebel
> Bending low I heard him say
> 'God bless my home in dear Cork city
> God bless the cause for which I die.'

Theresa   I hate the fact I came from between your legs.

Angela *hangs her head in shame.*

Theresa *comes and embraces her.*

Blackout.

Scene Ten

On the road.

Michael *and* **Liliane** *are trekking towards Liverpool and the sunset in the west. They suddenly have a view down towards the city. It is being pounded by bombs. There are fires everywhere.*

Liliane   Look at that.

Michael   Like one giant bomb's gone off –

Liliane   The city is on fire.

Michael   This is it – it's burnin' down –

Liliane   I can't believe my eyes – everything – the horizon is on fire –

Michael   The sun's landed on top of the Liver Birds – meltin' every'n' down –

Liliane   Look! There! – you see the planes?

Michael   Jesus, they're fast.

Liliane   There's one down –

Michael   Into the river. Dead man. Drownin' while he burns.

D'yer know what. Never shoulda come back. Me and J should've 'alf-inched a boat when we had the chance, set a course for somewhere. Woulda been rough for the first few days like, but we'd a-gotten used to it. Headed for Africa or wherever, bag ourselves a desert island, like what's-is-name – Start again, know wharra mean? What's the big idea about this place anyway, ey? Great fuckin' Britain.

Liliane   Michael –

Michael   The Nazis'll be all over it like flies on shit soon enough, won't thee? Far as I'm concerned, they're fuckin' welcome to it –

Liliane   Listen.

Michael   What. What is it?

He realises.

Gettin' off, are yer. Can't say's I blame yer, I'm not much
company –

Liliane   Thank you. And J.

Michael   What for.

Liliane   For looking after me.

Michael   Yer just gonna get off – like that? Yer serious.

Liliane   I'm grateful.

Michael   I thought – thought you'd want to come with us –
after, like –

Liliane   From here – your path is not my path.

Michael   We could get yer to Ireland or the Lakes or
wherever –

Liliane   Do you understand what I am saying?

Pause.

Felix always wanted to go to Ireland. He was very romantic
about it. He read too many poems about dark-eyed girls, and
death, and the hungry sea. He was romantic about everything.
He had been in the camp for six weeks before I found him. We
could talk together through the wires, they didn't mind. I knew
straight away I would never have him in my arms again. There
was death in his face, in his voice. Standing and speaking, but
he was in the grave.

Michael   Come with us.

Liliane   I can't.

Michael   Why not?

Liliane   You know.

Michael   It's not safe for yer –

Liliane   This is my problem.

Michael   It won't be if you come with us –

Liliane (*talking over him, insistent*)   This thing you want to do – it is not my path.

Michael   It isn't – it's not so black and white, you know –

Liliane (*forcefully*)   Yes, I am afraid it *is*. So black you cannot see. So white you cannot hide.

This time it's she who is upset and he can't comfort her.

Michael   You'll be alright.

Liliane   I hope so.

Michael   We could still see yer after –

Liliane   As I say –

Michael   See yer OK –

Liliane   Different paths.

Pause.

I'm glad we met.

Pause.

Michael *puts out his hand for* **Liliane** *to shake, she walks past it and embraces him.*

Liliane   Remember me –

She runs away.

Michael *heads off in the other direction.*

Scene Eleven

Michael's *wake.* **Phelan, Theresa, Angela, Colin, JJ, Father Quiggan.**

All are the worse for drink, except **JJ**. *Everyone is smoking.*

*They sing, as a rabble, a sentimental Irish song. The song finishes and the
assembly reach for their drinks and smokes.*

Phelan *grabs at* **Angela**, *who resists.*

Angela   Get off − That'll do −

Phelan   Not from where I'm standin' −

Angela   Tell him, Father.

Father Quiggan   What should I tell him, now.

Angela   Tell him it's me son's wake and he should be a bit
more, y'know −

Phelan   It's nearly over, isn't it − ?

Angela   Respectful.

Phelan   And sure no one ever smiled at a wake. What about
you, Theresa?

No response.

Your mother declines to oblige me. Come on over and give us
a kiss now with them ruby reds. I'm dyin' here. I'm an old man
in need of a kiss from his favourite girl.

Theresa   Are yer now.

Phelan   Nothin' funny about it, is there. I think of yer as me
own daughter, so why should I be ashamed?

Theresa   I'm not your bloody daughter.

Phelan   JJ − come 'ere, lad. Come 'ere while I ask yer.

Theresa   Don't be askin' him to fight yer battles.

Phelan   I know yer sweet on the girl − talk some sense into
her for us, will yer. Bit o' daughterly affection, then I'll hold me
peace.

JJ   Not a lot I can do for yer there, Mr Phelan.

Phelan   A little peck, now −

Theresa   Come near me, I'll swing fer yer.

Phelan   Ah, honest to God, she's an 'ard knock when she wants to be.

Theresa   Kiss you, I'd throw up.

Phelan *and* **Colin** *laugh over-loudly, clink their glasses.*

Phelan   I well remember the pukin' and mewlin' this one did when she was an ankle-biter!

Angela   God, don't – Was up to me eyes in it mornin', noon and night –

Colin   Bet yer was, as well –

Angela   Our Michael was no better, mind, he could shit for Ireland, that one. Yer'd no sooner done a boil-wash than there was another pile o' nappies stinkin' to high heaven –

Father Quiggan   A mother's work is never done.

Angela   Never a truer word. Poor Eileen won't know what's hit her. Ey, Vin, what yer playin' at?

Phelan   What have I done now?

Angela   Father's glass is empty there.

Phelan   Ey. Can't have that. Guinness you're on, is it, George – ?

Father Quiggan   I won't say no.

Phelan   John?

JJ   I'm alright, Mr Phelan.

Phelan   You sure now?

JJ   I'm fine, honest.

Phelan   I'll get yer one all the same. No sense in runnin' dry. Theresa, yer alright? Colin! Ready for another?

Colin *gestures 'yes'.*

Exit **Phelan**.

Colin   Got a lovely voice on yer, Theresa.

Theresa   You talkin' to me?

Colin   Was only sayin' –

Theresa   What. Sayin' what, monkey.

Angela   Arr ey, girl, leave the lad alone –

Colin   Just sayin', she's got a really nice singin' voice.

Angela   She never could take a compliment.

Theresa   Depends who's givin' it.

Colin   Ah, that's not nice.

Theresa   Listen – not bein' funny, but what are you still doin' here? Hangin' round like a bad smell. If it weren't for the fact Father's here, tellin' yer –

Colin   What? Tellin' me *what*?

Angela (*woozy, slurring her words*)   Take no notice to her, lad.

Colin   No skin off *my* back, Mrs D – you feelin' OK there?

Theresa   Had one over the eight, haven't yer, Ma. She can't control herself.

She turns away.

Enter **Phelan**, *with bottles of drinks.*

Phelan   Aye aye, Ange – can't take yer ale, is it?

Angela   I'm alright. Going outside for a breath.

She exits.

Phelan   What's all this?

Colin   She's sayin' I shouldn't be here.

Phelan   Ah, the bark's worse than the bite –

Colin   Just as well.

Phelan   Met their Michael loads o' times, haven't yer, practically yer bezzie mate, wasn't he?

Theresa   Yer what?

Colin   Played snooker with him more than once.

Phelan   Case closed.

Colin   Thank you.

He gestures towards **Father Quiggan.**

Colin   She's sayin' if it wasn't for him she'd tell me where to go.

Theresa   You are one annoyin' get, d'yer know that?

Phelan   You'll not get any sense out of him, girl – He's a nutcase, this one.

He leaves them to it.

Colin   It's hypocritical, to me.

Theresa   That's a big word. All's I'm gonna say to you – Ah, what's the point . . .

Colin   I'm only messin' with yer, queen. Saw yer talkin' to him –

Theresa   Who?

Colin   The sky-pilot –

Theresa   Priest.

Colin   The way you were lookin' at him –

Theresa   What way.

Colin   I don' know. Amazes me how they can be, y'know, how they can go their whole lives without – y'know – without scratching the itch.

Theresa   It's called goodness. Holiness.

Colin   Whatever it is, I can't work it out – why they do it, like. Here he is now, think I'll ask him.

Father Quiggan *joins them.*

Father Quiggan   I'm not interrupting.

Theresa   I was just sayin' to Colin, you've known me all my life, haven't yer?

Father Quiggan   Now doesn't that make me feel the old man –

Angela *enters.*

Theresa (*forcefully*)   Father Quiggan's baptised me, confirmed me, heard me confessions –

Colin   That right, yeah – ?

Theresa   Yes. It *is* –

Angela   Still on yer case is she, lad?

Theresa (*raising her voice*)   And he's buried me dad, hasn't he! He buried my father – D'yers remember? Remember, Ma? Cemetery all white with the frost. Bitter bleedin' wind blowin' in from the sea. The undertakers were in a state cos the boss's lad just been listed missin'. And there's me dad in a box, what's left of him. Father sent him on his way with a shake of the holy water. Now it's Michael's turn, isn't it. Who's next, d'yers think? Who's next, ey?

Father Quiggan   These are dangerous days.

Pause.

Colin   I bet you've heard some things in yer time, ey, Father? In confession, like.

Father Quiggan   You could say that, lad, aye. Some daft things and some dreadful things.

Colin   All them sins. They all get forgiven, do they?

Father Quiggan   If the sinner's truly sorry, yes, they are.

Colin   Anyone can say they're sorry, though, can't they. People'll say all kinds if they think they can get away with it.

Angela   Yer've 'ardly touched yer pint, John Joe, love.

JJ   Not used to the sauce, am I. Got a long walk back, as well.

Angela   Well, you're always welcome to kip on the couch at ours, lad, you know that.

JJ   Thanks a lot, yeah.

Angela   Any time you want, you know.

JJ   I know, thanks. Appreciate that.

Angela   What'll yer do now.

JJ   Now?

Angela   In the next few weeks.

JJ   Oh, don't know. Some decent kip'd be nice.

Phelan   You'll be lucky, lad.

Angela   Sirens goin' every five minutes.

Father Quiggan   I always find a little nightcap helps.

Colin   Oh aye, Father.

Father Quiggan   Drop of the hard stuff, and I'm away.

Phelan   The sleep of the just, ey? Talkin' of which –

He raises his glass.

Here's to Michael.

All   To Michael.

Angela   God keep him.

Father Quiggan   May the Lord God bring you the comfort of his peace.

Phelan   He was a good lad, never any trouble to his mother and father. Died fighting for what he believed in. He's died a good death.

Angela (*and others*)   Amen.

JJ   Amen.

All drink in silence for a while.

Angela *starts a mournful rendition of 'Love's Old Sweet Song'.*

Angela
Once in the dear, dead days beyond recall,
When on the world the mists began to fall,
Out of the dreams that rose in happy throng,
Low to our hearts love sang an old sweet song,
And in the dusk where fell the firelight gleam,
Softly it wove itself into our dream.

Just a song at twilight, when the lights are low;
And the flick'ring shadows softly come and go
Tho' the heart be weary, sad the day and long,
Still to us at twilight comes love's old song,
Comes love's old sweet song.

Even today we hear love's song of yore,
Deep in our hearts it swells for ever more.
Footsteps may falter, weary grow the way;
Still we can hear it at the close of day.
So till the end, when life's dim shadows fall,
Love will be found the sweetest song of all.

When she's finished, the assembly break into applause.

Phelan   That's lovely that, queen.

JJ   Really nice, Mrs D.

Angela   Thanks.

Colin   Never heard it sung with more, what would you call
it . . . ?

Phelan   Heart of a lioness, this one.

Father Quiggan   Truly beautiful.

Colin   Feeling.

Phelan   God's honest truth.

Angela   Be quiet.

Theresa *is crying.*

Phelan   Singin' for her Michael.

Father Quiggan   There's a consolation in music.

Slight pause.

Phelan   'Ere y'are, John Joe, get our Theresa up, will yer. I can't abide to see her gorgeous face so miserable. Get her up, lad.

JJ   If she wants to, Mr Phelan, but erm –

Phelan   Theresa, queen, come on now. Yer've cried an ocean for yer father, only right and proper, and yer'll give Michael his due, I know yer will. But here now, let JJ take you for a slowie, forget yerself for a wee while, why not.

Theresa   I'm not dancin' for you, alright?

Phelan   Ah, but sure, this is yer brother's right-hand man that's askin' yer, the last livin' soul that looked on him.

Theresa   He's fine fer dances, aren't yer.

Phelan   What d'yer say, John Joe.

JJ *stands, offers his hand to* **Theresa***.*

JJ   I will if she will.

Pause.

Phelan   No good. Stuffin' knocked out of 'er, know wharra mean.

Pause.

Theresa *stands, takes* **JJ***'s hand. They begin a slow, courtly dance. Eventually, he decides the time is now.*

JJ   You alright?

A tearful laugh.

Theresa   Never better.

Pause.

Coulda done with yer here with me.

JJ Here now, aren't I.

He pulls her closer.

Can I ask you something?

Theresa If you like.

Pause.

Why're yer lookin' at me like that.

JJ Are you any good at keepin' a secret.

Theresa Don't know. Depends.

JJ How d'you mean.

Theresa If it's a big one, I'm pretty good. If it's important.

JJ If it's a little one.

Theresa More than likely I'd let it slip. That answer yer? So what is it.

JJ I lied.

Theresa Yer what – ?

JJ Michael got yer letter. He's back.

They continue dancing as the scene dissolves around them. The music transforms itself to something triumphant and assertive. **JJ** *exits.*

Alone with the music, **Theresa** *contemplates revenge.*

Scene Twelve

Recognition.

Theresa *and* **JJ** *in Anfield Cemetery, to meet* **Michael**.

JJ Are yer alright?

Theresa What do *you* think. I'm a bag o' nerves.

JJ   He's your brother.

Theresa   I know that, soft lad. Thought he was gone, that's all. Like meetin' a ghost.

JJ   I know.

Theresa   This woman. What's 'er name.

JJ   Lili.

Theresa   You trust her, do yers.

JJ   She's a peach – don't you worry about her.

Theresa   No?

JJ   Reminds me o' you.

Theresa   Oh aye. Nark is she. Pain in the arse.

Short pause.

JJ   Time, I think.

Theresa   I'm scared, J.

JJ   Don't be, sweetheart.

He takes her by the shoulders, pulls her round for an embrace.

Theresa   If he's here – It's too much.

Michael *approaches.*

JJ   Be alright, you'll see. Don't cry now. Don't, girl. You'll be alright.

Theresa   Yer promise?

JJ   Promise.

Michael   Promise.

Brother and sister are face to face in the dark. So she says to him:

Theresa   Don't make promises you can't keep, brother o' mine.

Michael   Can't see yer face.

Theresa   Just as well.

Michael   Why d'yer say that.

Theresa   Crybaby, aren't I.

Michael   What for, soft girl.

Theresa   Not for you –

Michael   For me dad.

Theresa   For her, if yer want to know. For me mam.

Michael   Yeah.

Theresa   Can't be helped, can it?

Michael   No.

Pause.

Theresa   Where the fuck've yer been.

Michael (*laughs*)   Yer what – ?

Theresa   You 'eard. Where the fuck've yer been.

Michael   I don't know. All over.

Theresa   Where.

Michael   Hell and back.

Theresa   Where.

Michael   France. Spain. Marrakesh.

Theresa   Bully for you.

Michael   Got your letter in the end, didn't I.

Theresa   He said. Just before Chrimbo.

Michael   Been on the road since then.

Theresa   You couldn't write.

Michael   Couldn't risk it.

Theresa   No. No. You gonna do it then?

Michael   Too right I am.

Theresa   Thought you might've gone off the idea. Gone soft.

He takes out the gun. She takes it briefly, hands it back.

Michael   'Aven't come back to shake his hand, Theresa.

Theresa   Say that again.

Michael   What.

Theresa   Me name.

Michael   Yer name – ?

Theresa   Say me name.

Michael   Theresa.

Theresa   Your voice, like me dad's.

Michael   Come here . . .

They embrace.

Theresa   We might not see her again.

Michael   After.

Theresa   Yer realise that.

Pause..

She'll hate us. The end of the day we're hers though, aren't we. She's ours. Flesh and blood.

Michael   Is right. What's he? Fuckin' piggy bank.

Theresa   They must've known there'd be comeback.

Beat.

Michael   What was the funeral like.

Theresa   Dad's or yours.

Michael   His.

Theresa What do *you* think? Just get to ours and get it over with, will yer. Been no kind of a life waitin' round here for you to get yer bleedin' act together, tellin' yer. Another week and yer'd've found me swingin' from the ceilin' –

JJ Shurrup, will yer –

Michael We'll get it done. Be alright.

Theresa Yers won't hurt me mam.

JJ No danger.

Michael Yer know the score. Yer let us in at three. If it's no go, someone's in the privy or whatever –

Theresa Do I look stupid to you. I've got it.

Michael Alright . . .

Another embrace.

See yer later.

JJ *and* **Michael** *melt away into the darkness.* **Theresa** *goes in the opposite direction.*

Scene Thirteen

The Donohue house, five to three in the morning, Grey dim light through the windows

Theresa *sits smoking, alone. She's not wearing night things. She is wracked. She checks the time, goes to the door, opens it and stands breathing the night air.*

Theresa Not yet. Oh Jesus. Don't want it yet –

Phelan *has appeared, stands watching her for a second, then:*

Phelan Don't want what yet.

Theresa *spins round, shocked.*

Theresa Fuck's sake.

Phelan   Some thunderstorm that was –

Theresa   What you doin' up?

Phelan   Glass o' water – what's your excuse.

Theresa   Been out walkin'.

Phelan   Oh aye.

Theresa   Go back to bed.

Phelan   Coppers'll think yer a tart. Or you'll get caught by a raid.

Theresa   No chance.

Phelan   No, that's it, not you. You're immortal, aren't ye.

Theresa   Just leave me in peace, will yer.

Phelan (*leaving, turns to say*)   You'll come round in the end. I'm not such a bad feller, am I, all's said and done. Get to bed now, save some o' them smokes for tomorrer.

When he's gone, **Theresa** *stands a few moments, then closes the door and sits down. The pressure on her is visible.*

Bombs land in the distance. **Theresa** *listens, rapt.*

Father Quiggan *appears to her.*

Father Quiggan   To wish for death is a sin, child.

Theresa   Oh, Father –

Father Quiggan   And if I were to tell you Michael will fail.

Theresa   What do you know about it.

Father Quiggan *shows her his wounds – his flank is a mess.*

Theresa   Mother o' Christ – !

Father Quiggan   Holy Cross was marmalised just now. The church, and my little house. I was eating bread and jam in the study. Don't be afraid.

Theresa Poor Father . . .

Father Quiggan No, child. Nothing poor about me.

Theresa So this is me now. Talkin' to ghosts.

Father Quiggan You need to know – I'm here.

Theresa No –

Father Quiggan Save yerself. Stay your hand.

Theresa Too late.

Father Quiggan The day they crowned you May Queen – you were what. Twelve and a half? Such a to-do with the veil, was there not. Because it was made of arl dusty net curtains, yer mam had forgotten to wash them. D'you remember that now?

Theresa Oh, Father . . .

Father Quiggan Yer were coughing yer guts up, sneezin' yer head off yer were, and there's your mother all embarrassed, Mrs Coghlan sniggerin' behind her handbag, all the girls feelin' ashamed for yer, not daring to laugh because for all that them sneezes were uncontrollable, you were watching them – Kitty and Patricia and Cathleen, watching them like a hungry hawk –

Theresa You gave me yer hanky.

Father Quiggan I did too, but the pity of it was, it was none too clean, and this was vinegar in the cut, was it not.

Theresa I threw it back at yer.

Father Quiggan *pulls a neat clean linen handkerchief from his pocket and holds it out to her. She does not move to take it.*

Father Quiggan Stay your hand, child. Or you are lost. Hear me. Lost. (*He blesses her.*) *Nomine patris, filii, spiritus sancti –*

A massive explosion, and **Father Quiggan** *is gone.*

Theresa *is shaken to the core.*

There is a picture or statue of the Virgin, on the wall perhaps. **Theresa** *looks as if she might pray to it, but changes her mind, cursing herself for weakness.*

Maybe she has a drink instead. Dutch courage. It's time. Braces herself. Goes to the door, opens it.

Michael *and* **JJ** *enter quickly, with intent.*

Michael   Alright?

Theresa   If you are.

JJ   OK.

Michael   God forgive us, ey, mate.

JJ   Yeah. One more for the charge sheet.

Michael *and* **JJ** *go to the bedroom, enter it.* **Theresa** *waits.*

Confusion of shouting and swearing and screaming. In among which:

Phelan   WHAT THE BLOODY HELL –

Michael   GET UP!

JJ   MOVE IT!

Angela   OH CHRIST.

JJ   HANDS BEHIND YER HEAD, YOU!–

Angela *is screaming, then:*

Angela   MICHAEL!

JJ   DO AS YOU'RE FUCKIN' TOLD.

Michael   PUT THIS ON.

Phelan   BOYS – BOYS –

Angela   OH JESUS CHRIST.

Michael   GET THE FUCK OUT THE BED. STAND UP.

JJ   KEEP THE HANDS UP.

Michael   FRONT ROOM. NOW!

Angela   OH SWEET JESUS.

Phelan   KEEP THAT FUCKIN' THING AWAY FROM
ME –

Michael   SHUT UP AND MOVE –

Angela   FOR THE LOVE OF GOD.

Michael   MOVE!

Phelan   YOU'LL SWING FOR THIS, LAD.

Michael   SHUT YER FUCKIN' WHINING.

They exit the bedroom, **Michael** *holding* **Phelan** *at gunpoint. He is
bleeding from a head wound.* **Angela***, wearing a nightgown, is being
held firmly by* **JJ**. **Angela** *sees* **Theresa**.

Angela   Theresa – ? Tell me this isn't happenin' – I'm havin'
one of me nightmares –

Michael *points the gun at* **Phelan**.

Michael   Ey.

He waves him to sit. He then passes the gun to **JJ**, *and approaches his
mother.*

Michael   Thought I was dead, did yer.

Angela   Oh God, yes, I did.

Michael   Must've been hard.

Angela   It was –

Michael   I've thought about yer a lot.

Angela   Why wouldn't yer –

Michael   Are you jokin' with me?

Angela   What d'yer mean, lad –

Theresa   Mother –

Angela   What?

Theresa   We know what yers did. I've heard yer bleedin' pillow talk, haven't I?

Angela   No. Theresa – no –

Theresa   Yers murdered him, didn't yer! Then yers burned his body like he was a dog, and pretended he'd been caught in a raid. Well, we're here to tell yer. Took Holy Communion last Sunday, didn't yer? Knelt down like butter wouldn't melt while the priest put the host on yer tongue –

The body of Christ. The blood of Christ.

Well, I've got news for yer, Mother – you're *damned*, d'you hear? D'you hear me?

Angela   Michael –

Michael   In the kitchen, Ma.

Angela   No – no, Michael –

Michael   For your own good.

Angela   Michael, no, you can't. If you do this –

Michael   He's killed me dad. All there is to it. Comeback.

Angela   In the heat of the moment it happened! Frank used to hit me, yer know that.

Theresa   Don't you *dare* –

Michael   We know he did. Got nothing to do with anything, has it.

Angela   Vinnie's never so much as wagged his finger at me –

Michael   I'll say it one more time, and after that there's no more. Nothing more to say. He's killed my father. So. Yer know. Take her the back kitchen, J.

JJ   Come on, Mrs D.

Dazed, **Angela** *allows herself to be led off by* **JJ**.

Phelan   You lay a fuckin' finger on 'er –

Michael *slaps* **Phelan** *down.*

Michael   What d'yer think he is, ey? Some kind of fuckin' animal –

Another hit.

Theresa   Say yer prayers, Phelan.

Phelan (*to* **Michael**)   You won't do it.

Theresa (*approaching* **Phelan**)   Oh won't he?

Phelan   He hasn't go the balls –

Theresa *hits him.*

Phelan   Friggin' coward, that's what he is –

Another hit. **Phelan** *is hurt.*

Michael   Not such a big man now, are yer?

Phelan   Look – if you're thinkin' about killin' me – serious, now, it's not worth it –

Theresa   Not worth it?

Phelan   Yers are good kids. What use are yers dead to your mam?

Michael   Not plannin' on gettin' caught, are we?

Phelan   The busies may not find yer, granted. But there's certain vested interests in my well-being. My associates'll come lookin' for yer. The money I'm making for them will be missed. And they won't be marchin' yer to a cop shop, know wharra mean?

Michael   Don't believe a word of it.

Theresa   Do it now.

Michael *readies the gun, aims –*

Theresa   Shoot.

– and freezes.

DO IT!

Michael*'s in agony.*

Phelan   He's frightened, poor lamb –

Theresa   Michael!

Phelan   Had a good war, did yer, lad? Happy days, ey, Mikey boy?

Theresa   Kill him!

Phelan   This your hero, is it? He's cracked – only fit for the funny farm –

Theresa   Michael – ? Come here – ! Give!

Theresa *takes the gun from* **Michael**.

Phelan   Waited for him all this time, and now look. Like havin' a dog and barkin' yerself.

Theresa   Shut the fuck up, you.

Phelan   What're you gonna do, shoot me?

Theresa *shoots.* **Phelan** *is hit between the legs, he screams in agony.*

Michael   Theresa! Theresa, no –

Theresa (*marvelling at what she's done*)   Blood – !

A cry from **Angela** *in the kitchen.*

Angela   Michael!

Michael   What have you done?

Theresa   Payback, isn't it –

Michael   You're my sister –

Theresa   Toss my father to one side like scraps for the dog? That'll fuckin' learn yer.

Phelan*'s trying to speak.*

Theresa   What's that?

Michael *backs away,* **Theresa** *approaches* **Phelan** *leans in to hear his whispers.*

Theresa   What yer tryin' to say? Hell? Yeah. Hell is right.

Angela *screams and sobs.* **Michael** *is appalled by his mother's cries.*

Theresa (*raising her voice to be heard off*)   Shut up, you! If you hadn't spread yer legs, me dad'd still be here, wouldn't he?

Michael   Theresa –

Theresa   What? Soft lad. What.

Michael   Finish him off, will yer – ?

Theresa   Oh, feelin' sorry for him?

Michael   Put him out his misery.

Theresa   Maybe we should get a doctor for him, ey?

Michael   Listen to me – That thing in yer hand – you should never've touched it.

Theresa   He was right, you *have* lost it, haven't yer?

Michael   The place I found it – if you'd've seen where it came from –

Theresa Me *dad*, Michael! This is about me *dad*, if you've forgotten.

Michael   Just –

Theresa   Well, thanks for bringing it me, anyway. Phelan. Phelan?

She aims at **Phelan***'s chest.*

Theresa   Look at me. That's it.

She shoots three times, taking her time to aim each shot . **Michael** *becomes more distressed with each. As the shots ring out, a cry from the kitchen . . .*

A pause.

Michael *sits on the floor.*

Theresa   JJ! JJ!

Michael   She can't see this. Don't make her.

Theresa   Her doing, isn't it. JJ!

Michael   Don't. Beggin' yer.

Theresa   You're pathetic.

Michael   Scared for yer –

Theresa   What yer on about. JJ! Get in here!

Theresa *goes towards the door to fetch in* **JJ** *and* **Angela**. *Before she reaches the door* **Angela** *stumbles in, like a sleepwalker. She carries a large, bloody kitchen knife before her.*

Two seconds while **Theresa** *realises what has happened.*

Theresa   No –

Angela   We're all dead now.

Theresa *goes to the back kitchen and finds* **JJ** *dead, stabbed through the heart. She screams and sobs . . .*

Angela *comes over to* **Michael***, crouches down and, still holding the knife, embraces him.*

Angela   Never loved anyone more than you – Baby boy. Always will be.

You've got to go. You know that. Far away. D'you hear me? Son? Michael?

He kisses her bloody cheek. Gets up and moves to the door.

Go on. That's it. Far as you can.

He goes, she can hardly bear it.

My baby –

Theresa *re-enters, her dress covered in* **JJ** *'s blood.*

Theresa   I loved him, you knew I did –

Angela   What next, girl. Or didn't you think this far.

Theresa *aims the gun at her mother.*

Angela   God forgive you.

Theresa God's not here, Ma, in case you hadn't noticed.

Pointing towards dead **JJ**, *off.*

Theresa And HE wasn't HERE for YOU. He wasn't here for YOU!

Angela Let me pass.

Theresa Yer what?

Angela To Our Lady.

Angela *walks past* **Theresa** *to where an icon or statue of the Virgin is set.*

Theresa Where'd Michael go?

Angela *holds the statue in one hand and the knife in the other.*

Theresa *(sees what this means)* Mother –

She makes a move towards her mother, but **Angela** *warns her off with the knife.*

Angela *(readying herself for suicide)*
Hail Mary, full of grace
The Lord is with thee –
Blessed art thou among women,
Blessed is the fruit of thy womb Jesus.
Holy Mary Mother of God, pray for us sinners
Now and at the hour of our death. Amen.

Hail Mary, full of grace
The Lord is with thee –
Blessed art thou among women,
Blessed is the fruit –

Theresa *is offering the pistol to* **Angela**.

A pause.

Angela *drops the knife, takes the pistol. She goes to embrace or kiss* **Theresa**, *who backs away.*

Angela *goes into the kitchen, still clutching the statue.*

Pause.

Pistol shot in the kitchen.

Theresa *starts to cry.*

A supernatural explosion.

The **Virgin** *has appeared. The* **Virgin** *is a frightening presence. Numinous. Daunting and imposing. Not benevolent or pretty. Perhaps faceless under her veil.*

Sounds of horror begin – as if a hellish engine is starting up.

Theresa   Oh God, oh God, oh God – Holy Mother of – Hail Mary – Hail Mary – Queen of the May –

You can wipe it all away, can't yer? Wipe it clean for us? What you do, isn't it?

You want me to pray?

The sounds get louder.

What do you want from me? Want me to say sorry, do yer? Apologise? What did you expect? What did you ever do for ME!

SAY SOMETHING!

The **Virgin** *opens her mouth and arms wide as if to sing – but only sounds of horror come out, a terrible mix of battle sounds, feverish laughter, Nazi rallies and music-hall nonsense. It builds, then stops abruptly with:*

Blackout.